Kayleigh-Ann Doran steps into the world of non-fiction with her debut book, *Can't Stomach It*—a raw, compelling narrative born from her relentless battle with an undiagnosed, debilitating illness. A passionate advocate for both physical and mental health, she shares her journey with unflinching honesty, illuminating the resilience, vulnerability, and fierce determination that defines her story.

When she is not writing, she documents her life on Instagram; @KaayleiighAnn. where she documents the highs and challenges of living with a disability, tending to her allotment, working as a nurse, her gym escapades and love of walking, especially with her beloved dog, Toby.

In Memorial

My grandparents, Bridget, Leo, Michael and Teresa—you are loved by all your family and very much missed; I wish we had longer together.

To Jake, Nicola, Brodie and all the others. I hope that by telling my story, your stories live on, too and that you are at peace.

Kayleigh-Ann Doran

CAN'T STOMACH IT

AUSTIN MACAULEY PUBLISHERS®
LONDON • CAMBRIDGE • NEW YORK • SHARJAH

All of the events in this memoir are true to the best of author's memory. The views expressed in this memoir are solely those of the author.

A CIP catalogue record for this title is available from the British Library.

ISBN 9781037111921 (Paperback)
ISBN 9781037111938 (ePub e-book)

www.austinmacauley.com

First Published 2026
Austin Macauley Publishers Ltd®
1 Canada Square
Canary Wharf
London
E14 5AA

Many Thanks

To my family:

Mum, Dad, Sarah and Keith. I would not be here today if it were not for you. I love you and thank you.

To my extended family and friends—the support you have provided my family has got us through the worst of it. I cannot thank you enough, and there are too many people to thank individually, so I hope this suffices.

To Lilly and Michelle. You have been there through my highs and lows. You have put up with my moans, supported me when I was down, and partied with me when I was not so down. Thank you for showing me normal.

To all doctors, nurses, supporting staff and fellow patients, past, present and future, thank you.

To my Dog Toby—I know you can't read this.

Note to the Reader

First thing I would like to say is thank you so much for giving me your precious time to read my story—even if you don't finish the book.

I always wanted to tell my story, but I never really knew where to start. We always kept the hospital paperwork over the years, and it mounted up. Every time I looked at it, it brought back memories of isolation and unhappiness; just looking at it felt overwhelming.

In 2020, during COVID, I was advised to shield. The isolation that it brought made me relive parts of my history, my illness history. I realised my history was affecting me and that I was traumatised by it.

I would do anything to avoid hospitals, until I was critically ill before I asked for help, and when I was admitted, I could not sleep. I was always on edge, and I would relive my traumatic events in my head with flashbacks and nightmares.

I was eventually diagnosed with complex post-traumatic stress disorder (C-PTSD) and though eye movement desensitisation and reprocessing (EMDR) therapy, narrative exposure therapy (NET therapy) and general counselling. I started processing my history.

I realised that I needed to own my story, and not let my history own me. It took a lot of therapy, medication and self-reflection.

It was not easy, but by going through my history—exposing myself to memories, which I wanted to forget; reminding myself of the light in the darkness, and most of all showing myself compassion (something that a therapist taught me, that I continue to be rubbish at, but I am getting there).

I started coming to terms with and accepting my past, but not letting it rule my life. The book has been a great source of reflection.

To be honest, I do not know if anyone will want to read my story. I needed to go through my story and allow my brain to process it, for no one else but me. So, if this book forevermore stays as a Word document, I will still be proud of my achievement, because I will have written my story, and I will have given my story a voice. My voice.

If I ever get published, it will probably be the most vulnerable I will ever feel, as it will be like my wounds will have been opened and shown to the public for anyone to read and judge.

Just reflecting on this feels scary and overwhelming, but in speaking my truth, I would like to impact individuals who may have similar stories: health care workers who want to reflect on their roles and health care. But most importantly, for people who are isolated, gaslighted or fighting healthcare and alone with their illness or disease.

I want you to know that you are not alone. Keep fighting, know your truth. You will get there.

To quote *Marigold Hotel*: 'If you're not there, it is not the end.'

I do want to add to the medical professionals or the soon-to-be medical professionals, if I am honoured enough for you to read this book, in what precious spare time you have.

This book is not anti-NHS or medical professionals at all, but this book is about what happens when people with health conditions are stuck in a medical grey area, where things are not clear-cut and the patient's needs/symptoms do not fit certain criteria.

It also highlights the importance that no matter how long you have been a doctor or healthcare professional, your knowledge will always have its limits, and to be humble about that.

So, dear reader, thank you for even getting this far! Thank you so much for letting me offload my trauma onto your eyes. I will see you on the other side.

Lots of Love,

Kayleigh

PS. Some names have been changed to protect identities.

* * * *

2004: The year my life turned upside down.

I had just started high school, a geeky, freckly, block-fringed year seven student, sporting an oversized brown blazer—yes. That was indeed the colour of our uniform, courtesy of the nuns.

I was embarking on a Catholic education in an all-girls high school in the suburbs of London. Super cool, I know (insert eye roll). Despite many talents, being cool wasn't one of them. Ironically, those freckles do become trendy in the future—when you're 30!

My family and I had just returned from a once-in-a-lifetime holiday in America, visiting Disneyland. We narrowly missed Hurricane Katrina by four days and felt incredibly fortunate to be home safely, watching the devastation unfold on TV.

The trip was filled with mishaps; I, being the clumsy and unlucky one, picked up an ear infection, sustained two injuries requiring the Disney first aiders, and, as the grand finale, found myself a mere meter away from being struck by lightning.

To this day, I still feel a bit anxious during lightning storms.

Despite these challenges, the holiday was *unforgettable*. The memories of swimming in the pool, witnessing the Disney finale show, drifting along the lazy river with my family, enjoying pizza for breakfast, and marvelling at the enormous portion sizes are etched in my mind forever.

Mum and Dad had saved diligently for this trip—taking advantage of this year—before they would have had to pay the adult price for me the following year.

On the flight home, I was sitting in front of a man who coughed and spluttered the whole journey. The 11-year-old little me had not noticed and sat engrossed in the in-flight entertainment. We had a fat box TV at home, and so I was amazed how they had fit the TV in the head of the chair in front.

My sister, Sarah, who was three years younger than me, was asleep on the seat next to me, with her part-rounded glasses squished onto the side of her face. She was leaning on Mum, who was sitting on her other side. My sister had fair skin, though tinged red (sunburn) following the holiday. We did not share the same number of freckles.

On my face, they were abundant; it was hard to see pale skin for freckles, whereas she only had one or two. We both had brown hair; mine thick with a mind of its own, needing a lion tamer to get into a hair band.

Sarah's hair was more delicate and ladylike, sitting politely on her shoulders. She also had a fringe. Mum had made us both had block fringes as she believed it would stop us getting wrinkles on our foreheads.

I cannot argue with that logic.

I was never a child particularly concerned with my appearance. Looks simply didn't bother me; I didn't compare myself to other kids. I existed in my own world, where fashion and fitting in were secondary.

Cleanliness was my primary concern. My energy was focused on doing other things: playing in the mud, dreaming of being an archaeologist, devouring books on dinosaurs and human biology, or exploring the local woods, searching for reptiles. That's just how I was, and I'm perfectly fine with it.

My mum, her short brown hair streaked with blonde highlights, had drifted off during another movie. The slight turbulence jolted her awake, and she readjusted her round glasses, her piercing blue eyes now alert.

Beside her, across the aisle, sat my dad. His naturally stern face was creased in concentration as he scratched his greying moustache, seemingly absorbed in his book. But I knew better. He was a terrible passenger, and I was sure his light blue eyes had scanned the same lines repeatedly, his focus fractured by the turbulence.

One hand gripped his book, the other a white-knuckled fist around the armrest. We didn't know it then, but Dad struggled with anxiety; years later, he'd be diagnosed with generalised anxiety disorder.

Back then, it was just *Dad being Dad*. He tried to mask it, but sometimes his anxiety overwhelmed him. Heights, open spaces, driving, loud noises—all were triggers. But despite his quirks, we loved him dearly.

In the days following the holiday, I experienced holiday blues and jet lag. I did not know whether I was coming or going for at least 48 hours; I was a mess! One minute, tearful as I was never going to have a holiday like it again, the next minute, asleep so deeply that only a prince would have broken the curse.

As the days moved on and school approached, Mum, Sarah and I started doing the last-minute preparations for my first day at high school.

* * * *

The year sevens started school, a day before everyone else. My understanding was that this was to acclimatise the young people, getting them ready for this big leap into high school. The morning started a lot like our usual mornings for primary school; Mum shouting at Sarah to get out of bed.

Sarah just rolled over in bed and went back to sleep. Me getting up, dressed, backpacked and breakfasted. Sarah had eventually gotten up and dragged herself downstairs, dressed but half asleep, to eat breakfast.

My aunty and maternal cousins had come over the day before, and Mum had told me to show my new uniform to Aunt. So, I had run upstairs to change, coming downstairs with my blazer buttoned up and my socks pulled up. My cousins proceeded to un-geek me.

They were a few years older than me and went to the same school that I was going to. They undid buttons and slouched my socks, reminding me to only carry my backpack over one shoulder, not both.

I needed that guidance!

The following morning, Mum, Sarah, and I got into the car. Mum dropped Sarah off at my aunt's, as she would be taking Sarah and the younger cousins to primary school, who started the same day as we did. Mum drove right up to my new school and got out with me.

She started walking me in—with some other mums, standing at the bottom of the school—she gave me a squeeze and planted a big kiss on my forehead, in front of all my new classmates.

Cringe—

Over the summer, we had been tasked to made a project about Trojans. I had created a folder filled with information and pictures. We found out that our whole year would be split into two: Greeks and Trojans.

We were then split further into classes of 25; my form was called Trojans One. We had a sports teacher as our form tutor. I would say she seemed scary, but my little year seven brain saw every teacher as scary.

My form was filled with some people I knew from primary school and a lot of new people, whom I looked forward to getting to know. We found that our team colour was purple and that our patron saint (you have to have one in a Catholic school) was St Monica.

A quick Google search would show you that she was the patron saint of alcoholics, victims of abuse, adultery, widows, mothers facing difficulty and the icing on the cake, wayward children.

The school itself used to be a beautiful old manor house. It was then converted into a boarding school and then a school. It had an old chapel and a swimming pool. There were some newer buildings adjacent to it, such as a sports area, a hall and music rooms.

The school was famous for being in a music video, and even though that happened many years before I was there, it was still talked about. There were ghost stories of a grey lady. You could ask anyone, and they would tell you that they knew someone who had seen the ghost.

Prior to starting school, we all took part in a multiple-choice exam to establish what classes we would be placed in. I found out that I was in the second top class for most subjects and the top class in math. This blew my mind, as in primary school, I was in the lowest group for everything.

I was put in special classes for individuals who needed extra help with English. My year 6 teacher, so frustrated with my writing, once drew lines across my book to made my writing neater.

I was unable to do any sort of mental math at all, and my spelling was atrocious, no matter how many spelling tests I failed, even after practising. So, after the first day of school had finished, I could not wait to tell Mum and Dad. They were so pleasantly surprised. I was on a complete high.

It actually turned out I had undiagnosed dyslexia, which I was diagnosed with later in life. The person who assessed me for dyslexia, as an adult, informed me that I had a high IQ. I just was unable to process it. Mum and Dad also had similar traits, and Sarah was also dyslexic. So, it was likely genetic...thanks, genetic gods! Sorry to the proof-readers, who read through this book.

In form, I was given a school diary and learnt that we had seven classes a day: three in the morning, then a break, two more, lunch, then two more before home time. The school was vast; there were so many halls and stairs, but I soon became familiar with the location of my classrooms.

I soon recognised and became friendly with the people in the register next to me, as all the teachers sat us in alphabetical order—*original*. There was one girl who did not really like me, but I thought my presence bothered her more than I was bothered by her ignoring me.

Unfortunately for her, she was right next to me in the register and was pretty much in my vicinity the whole day.

She did warm up to me eventually, and we laughed about it in later years.

Each day I was there, it was exciting. Meeting all my new teachers, learning what we would be doing over the next year. Getting to know all these new people. It was positive and a little overwhelming, but I was coping and looked forward to a new day.

As the rest of the school returned from their holidays, the school breathed to life, and it was two weeks of bliss, happiness, fresh starts and coughing.

* * * *

Coughing, was that a typo?

I wish. As the school breathed to life, breathing for me became difficult *(see what I did there)*. I developed a cough. At first, I hardly noticed it. Over the next week, I started noticing it. Then over the third week, I definitely noticed it.

I began feeling worse and worse. By week three, it was a problem. My cough sounded suspiciously similar to the man who sat behind me on the plane—*Mum was convinced that was where I caught it.*

I was soon struggling to walk upstairs, as there were thousands at my school. I found sleeping flat almost impossible without feeling as though I was suffocating. Mum started to worry too.

My mum was a qualified nurse, and she seldom let us off sick. She was of the mindset that unless you had a fever, you were not ill, and unless something was visibly deformed, no A&E. There were flaws to this logic. When I was 11, I ran into a concrete step barefoot, breaking it.

Mum, keeping to her rules, told me that it would improve over the next few days and to power through the pain. The next few days, I just happened to be at a dance and activities play scheme.

I was very quickly unable to participate in it, and soon after, could no longer walk on it. She took me to A&E, where the lovely doctor told us that it was broken. A fractured metatarsal.

Anyway, by the Thursday of week three, Mum decided I was ill enough to stay off school sick and, that morning, she took me to my GP.

It was a time when you could call your GP and get a same-day appointment. Not like now, where getting a GP appointment is survival of the fittest.

My GP, whom I had seen many times with sprains and bumps and random rashes, listened to my chest and diagnosed me with bronchitis. He prescribed me antibiotics, inhalers and requested a chest X-ray.

So that morning, Mum drove me to our local hospital for a chest X-ray. I spent the rest of the week lying on the couch under my duvet watching daytime telly, snoozing, coughing, and generally feeling sorry for myself.

Unfortunately, the first course of antibiotics did not work, and I was given two further courses before my symptoms started improving. I was out of school for around two weeks, and whilst my fellow students were learning what a mood board is—*something to this day I still have absolutely no idea what it is.*

I was confined to rest at home with Mum, looking after me on her days off, and Grandma taking her two buses from Brixton Hill to visit me. Dad would also chip in with child care, but it was harder for him, as he worked full-time in an office and would need to travel to work.

My grandma and granddad were typical Irish grandparents. They both had blue eyes. Their once brown hair had now whitened, and in my granddad's case, thinned. My grandma loved cooking and feeding people; her clothes were always neat, and she had a particular smell. Grandma's smell.

Her hair was perfectly curled on top of her head and short. Never one hair out of place. My granddad, dressed like granddads of the day, would not leave the house without his hat and smart coat. Mum tells me that when she was young, he was a strong, stoic man, but by the time he had become a granddad, he had mellowed.

My maternal grandma and grandad had moved to England, from Ireland, separately to make a life for themselves and had met, married and along came my uncle and Mum. My maternal grandmother was born in a village on a picturesque island off Ireland, Achill Island, *which is my favourite place in the world.*

My granddad's parents lived on the outskirts of a town on mainland Ireland, and both grew up in poverty, but I never heard one complaint—they just got on with things and that was their way. My granddad and grandma doted on all their grandkids, and we loved them back so much.

They always made sure we had our bellies full—with porridge, cabbage and bacon or carrageen moss—when we visited them every Sunday.

Looking back now, we were very lucky to be able to have a grandma come over to look after us. Especially as she did not have the best health, and if she caught my bronchitis, she could have become very ill. Thankfully, she did not.

I was soon able to put that beautiful brown uniform back on and return to school. It felt like I had missed nothing, and I caught up with everything very quickly, all bar mood boards, *still no idea!* I had made friends that I was hanging out with at lunch, and went back to enjoying school.

* * * *

On Sunday, about a week later, Mum drove Sarah and me for the hour-long journey to Brixton Hill to visit our grandparents. Grandma welcomed us at the front door with the biggest of Grandma hugs. The house smelled of Grandma and Granddad with a hint of cabbage and bacon—*my favourite*.

We met Grandad in the living room, sitting in his chair. Mum and Grandma chatted away, and Grandad sat reading the newspaper. When Mum and Grandma took a breath, I updated Grandma with everything at school, and Sarah then did the same.

Grandma ushered us to the dinner table, and we sat around it. The dinner table only comfortably fitted two, but the four of us squeezed around it, whilst Grandad ate in the kitchen.

I don't know why he never ate with us, but it was what happened.

Mum, Sarah and I inhaled our dinner, and what little scraps remained would go on a plate, which would go out the front of the house, to feed the local feral cats.

After dinner, with our bellies full, we moved onto the sofa. I always sat on the left of Grandma with my head on her shoulder, breathing her in, slightly snoozing and allowing the cabbage and bacon feast to digest in our stomachs.

Grandma and Mum continued talking. Sarah and I would sit listening, butting in on occasion. Grandad would come in from the kitchen and sit on his chair, continuing to read the paper.

I secretly thought he enjoyed listening in, but as chatting was a girly thing to do, he would not admit to it.

I excused myself to go to the toilet, where I proceeded to effortlessly vomit everything I had just eaten, before returning to Grandma's left-hand side, as though nothing had happened.

* * * *

It's weird to vomit, let alone vomit effortlessly and even more to not made a fuss over it. However, for me, vomiting was so normal, it was like a non-issue. See, I had a long history of gastro-oesophageal reflux disease or reflux.

From birth, I was always hard to feed. I was fussy, and I would regurgitate my food. Mum tried her hardest, trying all the guidance and old wives' tales with no improvement. I was a ticking time bomb, it was, *when would she vomit*, not *if*. At family gatherings after feeding, I would be handed around the room, like I was about to explode: Whom would I vomit on first?

I was a problem child. At 6 months, I was kicked out of my childminder. I would love to say something cool, like I was a rebel child, such as Tommy from Rugrats. *What a reference*. The issue with this was that I had more of the personality of Chucky *from Rugrats, not the horror movie that would be a very different book!*

The real reason I was kicked out of the child minders was that I vomited too much, and this was too much of a handful.

Mum tells me that the childminder said it would be easier to look after two additional children than one of Kayleigh.

At the time, Mum was juggling being a nurse, teaching students, and being a student as well. My dad was working full-time, and they had to manage a baby whose milk did not want to stay in her stomach.

Mum likes to remind me that once she was teaching students and every time she turned to the blackboard on the wall, they laughed. Unbeknownst to her, she had baby vomit all down her back.

You're welcome, Mum!

When I was about 8 months old, as the first-born child to Rose and Vince (Mum and Dad), they could wait no longer and travelled over to see family in Ireland, to show me off. This particular time, we were staying with my grandma's family in Achill Island. My family were sitting in the living room with the turf fire blazing and the aroma filling the room.

Family from across the island had popped in to visit, and everyone squeezed into the living room. There were not enough seats, but somehow, we made it work. I had just been fed and was being passed around the room like a hot potato.

My great-aunt was cooing at me, and I vomited over myself and her, like something out of the exorcist. Mum came over and started cleaning up, but she noted that there was blood in my vomit. My Great Aunty noted it too and advised Mum to get me looked at.

Once we had returned home from Ireland, Mum took me to the GP the next day. The GP was also concerned; she advised Mum to take me to A&E, where they would be waiting for me, with the plan of having investigations.

Mum took me straight to the hospital, and Dad met us there with an overnight bag that he packed, with careful and thorough guidance from Mum.

* * * *

The hospital was an old Victorian building that was falling down around the people who worked there. Its white walls were greying and crumbling. When entering the building, it had a strange smell, a mixture of staleness, dampness and medicalness.

Cobwebs grew on the inside of the wooden windows that had been painted shut to stop people from falling out of them. As it was December, Christmas decorations had been scantily placed around the hospital. However, they had seen better days, with half-broken Christmas tree ornaments and sparsely placed tinsel, holding up the Christmas tree.

I was admitted to the children's ward. I was only there for a few days. I was nursed in a single room; this was due to an outbreak of meningitis on the ward. 12 children had been diagnosed with it, and two children, a brother and sister, passed away. Throughout the admission, Mum did not leave my side.

I was whisked away for multiple investigations, and the outcome of this was that I was diagnosed with gastro-oesophageal reflux disease. Over the next three days, I was trialled on medication and thickened fluids; the combination seemed to work, and I was discharged home.

Gastro-oesophageal reflux disease, otherwise known as reflux or GORD/GERD if you're American, is a condition where the stomach acid in the stomach flows back up into the food tube, otherwise known as the oesophagus.

This can be caused by a hernia in your stomach, which increases pressure, a poor muscle between the oesophagus and stomach, or triggering foods like spicy food, smoking or obesity. The symptoms include heartburn, vomiting, bad breath and weight loss.

* * * *

After my discharge, it was not long to wait before Christmas came. Mum, Dad and I celebrated our first Christmas at home as a new family of three. Mum had put an artificial tree up in our living room and decorated it with multi-coloured lights and traditional Christmas ornaments.

We still use the same ornaments to this day. However, the number of ornaments has grown over the years, with all the additional handmade ones from school, fetes or brownies.

Mum and Dad also decorated the room with a newly brought nativity scene, *which we also continue to use, although we have lost a king, the shepherd was no longer attached and the Angel Gabriel has to be balanced on the roof of the stable at an angle, to stop him from falling to the ground—the Angle Gabriel.*

On Christmas Day, Mum dressed me up in a flouncy dress—*because this was what you did in the 90s*—we had Christmas Day breakfast, and at 10:30 am we left for church. For my parents, church was very important. They have been a part of a congregation at a Catholic church since before I was born. Together, they joined the church choir, where my dad played guitar/bass and my mum sang.

To this day, they continue to be a part of this church choir. Through the church, they have made friends and gained a supportive community.

After mass, my dad helped put away the musical instruments whilst Mum showed me off to people in the congregation, whom she had not seen for a while. When this was finished, we travelled home, where Mum started cooking a Christmas Day roast, turkey, the trimmings and a pudding.

I obviously was still on the thickened milk and some chewy foods. My dad drove the hour to Brixton Hill, where they lived, to pick up my maternal grandparents and bring them to our house to share in the Christmas Day feast.

In the late afternoon, the five of us travelled the five minutes over to my maternal uncle and aunt's house, where we exchanged gifts and shared further Christmas Day celebration, which was mostly lots of chatting and watching of Christmas Day TV. Early into the evening, my grandparents were driven home, and we soon departed for home too.

At the time, my maternal uncle and aunt had two girls, one two years older than me and one 10 months older than me. My Aunty and Uncle went on to have two more boys, the first was born one month before Sarah and the second, eight years later.

Both Sarah and I were very close to our cousins when growing up. My aunt also supported Mum with childcare throughout our childhood. It was so nice to have family who we were close to, not only physically, but socially, as well as in age.

The weird period of no man's land, between Christmas and New Year, was filled with social events. My mum had annual leave and she pottered about tidying the house from the Christmas celebration, whilst simultaneously looking after me.

As well as meeting up with friends and family. My dad, who at this time was working as a solicitor, continued to work. He always found it very hard to switch off and would work all the hours God gave him, if he could.

* * * *

The New Year soon came around, and the plan was that Mum, Dad and I would travel up to Borehamwood to visit my paternal family. My dad was one of four, two sisters and one brother; they were brought up in and around Northumberland and Newcastle.

All the siblings moved down south, but the grandparents stayed up north and settled in Northumberland. Unfortunately, they were unable to travel down this New Year's, so we wished them a Happy New Year through a phone call.

One of Dad's sisters worked as a speech and language therapist. They went on to have two boys, one a year younger than me and one 10 years younger than me. She was tall, thin, with a friendly smile and dark brown hair just like my dad's.

His other sister worked as a psychologist and, in later years, went on to get a doctorate. She had two girls, one three years older than me, who went on to live in Canada. The other, who was one year younger than me, went on to live in North London.

Like her sister, she had dark hair, was tall, thin, but although she was not the eldest of the siblings, she was the mother figure. When I was younger, I would struggle to tell the sisters apart as they looked alike, and when I saw them, they were always together.

Dad's brother was a tall man with dark brown hair and blue eyes; he looked a lot like Dad without the moustache. Before I was born, he got married and went on to have two girls. Unfortunately, around this time, he was diagnosed with schizophrenia, which, even with medication, required support.

This, as you may understand, complicates a family dynamic. He continued to be very much loved in our family and attended most family events.

*A*s an extended family, we saw the new year in, although I slept through it being a baby. *When asked, my mum and dad could not recall the finer details, but knowing my family, it would involve food, lots of chatting and general joy and happiness. My aunt always created a feast when we visited.*

We travelled home on New Year's Day, and following the Christmas period, things started returning to normal. Dad continued working, and Mum returned to work and her studies. I continued to vomit, but it was much more manageable.

* * * *

Over the next few days, I became ill. Nothing specific, just that I was under the weather with a fever and general malaise. However, I was not getting better, so Mum took me to our GP. Initially, they thought it may be German measles (rubella); however, once the GP undertook an assessment, she told Mum that I needed to go to the hospital straight away.

Following the doctor's recommendations, Mum took me to the hospital. It was the same hospital that I had previously been admitted to. Prior to our arrival, the GP had informed the hospital. . On entering, I was whisked off into paediatric resus, where I was poked and prodded and underwent many tests.

Whilst these tests were being undertaken, Mum was brought into the relative's room, and when my dad arrived at the hospital, he joined her until the doctors finished their testing. My parents at the time were very relaxed; why would they be anything else?

They were under the impression that I had rubella. They believed we were being separated to give the health care professionals space, not that I was critically unwell.

Eventually, a male doctor and nurse came into the relative's room, closed the door and sat down opposite my parents.

'Mr and Mrs Doran, it is nice to meet you abet the circumstances. Your GP was right to advise you to come here.' He took a breath and continued, 'Unfortunately, our test confirmed that Kayleigh has meningococcal septicaemia.'

He paused again, allowing Mum and Dad to process the gravity of the situation.

‘At this point, she has a 50% chance of living, but we are doing everything we can do. The next stage is to transfer her to a specialist hospital in London. At this hospital, she will get around-the-clock specialist care by people who are the best in their speciality.’

When I spoke to Mum about this event, she remembered everything that was said, but she reported that she just didn’t truly believe I was that ill, and because of this, was not worried.

The doctor went on to say, ‘Everyone who has been in contact with Kayleigh, whilst she has been infectious, will need to be prescribed antibiotics as a health prevention precaution.’

This included all my cousins, aunties and uncles with whom I had spent New Year’s.

My aunt blames the antibiotics given to one of my cousins as the reason she had wonky teeth.

The ambulance arrived with two specialist paediatric ITU paramedics. Due to the situation, they had PPE and were dressed in space suits. I was loaded onto the ambulance with wires and tubes coming out of me, and I was rushed to the specialist hospital on blue lights. My poor dad had to try and follow the ambulance in his silver Astra—lucky for him, speed cameras were not a thing at that time.

When we arrived, I was taken into a side room and the medical professionals hooked me up to machines, started me on antibiotics and fluids.

Mum recalls that everyone was very relaxed and not worried, which further supported her in not being particularly worried.

In the days following the admission, my mum got into the routine of the ward, and each day I continued to improve.

The biggest spoiler alert that I didn't die was the fact that I am writing this book.

Mum stayed by my side throughout, and Dad tried to get in as often as work would allow. My mum and dad were supported throughout this time by family over the phone and the staff on the ward.

About day 8 of my admission, my dad travelled up to the ward. He came into the room and gave me a kiss on my cheek and a hug to Mum. They sat down together, and Mum started to update him on what had happened over the day on the ward. Dad then updated Mum on all the things happening at home.

A nurse knocked on the door and entered. She informed Dad that he had received a call on the ward phone. This was not normal; in fact, no one had ever called him through the hospital switchboard before. Both Mum and Dad were intrigued. Dad got up and followed the nurse out of the room and to the phone.

In the in-between, Mum fussed over me, and about 3 minutes later, Dad came into the room. Shutting the door behind him, he was pale, clammy and shakily sat down.

He looked up and into Mum's eyes, and just said, 'My mum has died.'

Mum and Dad sat in silence together; they were both completely shocked. Her death was completely out of the blue. She had not been ill, and although she smoked, there was no precursor to her death.

Dad then made the heartbreaking decision of leaving his sick daughter in a London hospital, who had been fighting for her life, or going up to Northumberland to support his family with the death of his mum. As I had been improving and was no longer critical, Mum and Dad made the decision that I was well enough for him to travel.

My grandma was in her late 60s. She had dark grey short curly hair with blue eyes, just like Dad's, and she had the most beautiful smile. I know she could appear stern and scary, which was probably a good thing as she had been a teacher.

Like Grandma, Granddad was also a teacher but had gone on to be a head teacher. He had white hair and was also blessed with blue eyes. He definitely gave off middle-class head teacher vibes with his neatly pressed shirts and general chattiness.

My paternal grandparents lived together in a bungalow in Warkworth, Northumberland, right around the corner from the castle. Dad used to tell me stories that Granddad was asked to play football for England, but he had declined this, as teaching paid more.

Granddad had also been conscripted in the war, where he was a radio operator. His brother (my great uncle) was in Dunkirk and was awarded the Legion of Honour from France.

Grandma was buried not far from Grandma and granddad's holidaying caravan. The graveyard was small but peaceful, surrounded by greenery, and it overlooked the stunning Northumberland coast.

My dad supported his siblings whilst staying in contact with Mum daily. My dad and our family were heartbroken.

After my discharge and once I was well enough, we travelled back up north to see the family. Dad told me that when we saw each other, Granddad gave me lots of cuddles, and although it did not fill the Grandma-sized hole in our hearts, as a family, we soldiered on.

My granddad passed away a year later from a broken heart. It was such a huge loss to our family and caused a chapter in our lives to close. My paternal grandparents both died too soon, but at least they knew they were very loved. They knew that we spent as much time as we could with them, with the distance, and that was the only silver lining.

* * * *

My earliest memories were as a toddler. Mum and Dad had eventually got me into a preschool as my eating had improved and, more importantly, my vomiting had declined, although not stopped. The nursery was a little 10-minute walk from our house. I had a friend called Ben, and we were like two peas in a pod, following and playing with each other.

Mum and Dad were informed that the building had been condemned and the preschool would be closing, so we left, waving goodbye to each other, never knowing if we would ever meet again.

A few years of sitting in ruin, the building was done up and became a synagogue and then a Hindu temple, so it could not have been too bad! I also never saw Ben again, but I vividly remember saying goodbye.

When I was 3, my mum and dad told me I was going to be a big sister. I could not wait. I don't remember being told about being a sister, but I remember that my maternal uncle and aunt agreed to look after me when Mum was in labour.

I was so excited. I could not sleep. My aunt removed me from my cousins' rooms and placed me in the living room to play with all the toys.

My dad picked me up the next day to take me to the hospital, where I got to meet my beautiful sister. Sarah was a nine-pound, brown haired, and I was in love. Mum and Dad gave me a present from Sarah, and I loved her even more.

I would like to take this time to apologise to my aunt and uncle for all the lack of sleep that night, especially as you had two children and a newborn to look after!

We were able to take Sarah home that day, and we became a family of four. The world, as I knew it, had changed for the better—*although don't tell her that!*

* * * *

Aged 4, I commenced primary education at the local Catholic primary school, which also happened to be connected to the church my parent were parishioners of. The school was a 15-minute walk and a 5-minute car journey away from our house. Mum liked the idea of walking and we did try to walk when we could, but it would depend on whether we were running late, the weather or work.

We were always running late. Mum, in general, goes by Irish time (always late), which drove Dad crazy, as he was always early. One holiday, he was so nervous about being late, we ended up getting to the airport 5 hours early. The plane was then delayed 3 hours!

The uniform, like most schools, was split into summer and winter. In the summer, the uniform was a blue, thinly checked dress and a grey jumper with a logo embossed. In the winter, it was a blue polo top, dark grey skirt and light grey jumper embossed with the school logo; the polo top became a shirt in key stage two.

Mum went a little rogue with the uniform instead of the skirt, and I would wear a grey pinafore. *Now imagine a pinafore, block-fringed freckly girl with curly piggy tails. I was a sight for sore eyes, a solid 8/10 on the cuteness scale and 10/10 on the geek scale.*

Our week would consist of swimming lessons on Thursdays after school, and on Saturdays, Sarah and I went to Irish dancing lessons.

On Saturdays, Mum would drop us off at dancing and Dad would pick us up. On the way home, Dad would take us to the sweet shop and we were given a pound each to spend, however, we wished. All before returning home to a Saturday afternoon house clean, and then food shopping in the late evening.

We would then get home, sit in front of the TV and have a takeaway, usually a curry—*my favourite!* We would bring our duvets downstairs, cosy up together and watch a movie before bed, blockbuster, when it was a thing before Netflix.

I was usually an early riser, and on Sunday mornings I would bring my duvet downstairs again and put Sunday Morning TV on. Dad and I would then go to church at 10:00 am to set up the choir, and Mum and Sarah would come at 11:02 am for the 11:00 am mass.

After mass, the church club would be open. Sarah and I would play in the garden, and Mum and Dad would catch up with all their friends. Every second Sunday, we would visit my maternal grandparents' house.

They would feed us, and I would cuddle up on my grandma's shoulder, listening to Mum and her talk about the week. Or Sarah and I would roam the house, playing games and scaring each other.

We would regularly see my maternal cousins, and because of our closeness in age and similar interests, we got on really well. Sarah was also in the same year at school as one of our cousins. We would also regularly get picked up from school by my aunty when my mum and dad worked long days.

When it snowed, my aunty would pick us up early from school and take us to her house. We would play there like feral children in the woods, and go sledging; some of my favourite childhood memories are of snow days.

When I was old enough, I started brownies. I was so proud, with my yellow jumper and brown joggers. I looked forward to brownies every week, excited to see what new and exciting activities we would be doing.

Although Mum and Dad created a routine and I should have been really content, it was around this time that I started to notice that I didn't really fit in anywhere. I didn't have close friends. I would go between the different friendship groups. I remember sitting alone at lunchtime or walking the lines of the netball court during break.

I felt alone, but I don't remember feeling particularly unhappy or depressed. However, my classmates soon noticed this, and I was picked on a fair amount. The only time the school intervened was when I got punched in the stomach by a boy in an older class.

He went on to be a police officer. To this day, I stay in contact with one person from primary school.

Music was my safe space. Not only was I brought up in a very musical household, but I was also very quick to learn, recorder and read music. I went on to study violin and, in later years, play piano. In year six, I was lucky enough to win a music award at our end-of-school awards.

At school, although I was not gifted in most sports, I was slower than everyone else when running and got easily injured. I was fairly tall and was placed in the netball team as goal attack. Only when the other girls started to catch up and outgrow me was I demoted to the B team.

My illness flared up occasionally over the years, and I would be given a course of medication to settle it. I was never mindful of what I ate, ever. I would eat a man-sized portion of spaghetti Bolognese and even more when it came to Indian.

I would be that child who would happily eat a third portion of food if it were tasty. I would just absorb the food, with the biggest smile on my face, if I vomited, well, that was just second then!

* * * *

When I was about 7, after years of being on and off the same medication. My GP wanted to check in, to make sure there was nothing else going on. So invited me to undergo investigations. It was very exciting, I got to have a half day at school, with Mum picking me up to go to the hospital for the test. I was leaving school early, and I was not even sick!

Mum and I drove to the local hospital, North Surrey Hospital, parked up and searched for radiology. We entered the waiting room. It had white walls and a light blue floor. I remember that it smelled like a hospital, too. There was a little kiddie section with toys and cartoons drawn on the walls.

We went to the reception, where I was given a gown, with hospital property written all over it in multicolours, which I got changed into. *I remember feeling very exposed, so I kept my school tights on.* Mum and I sat in the waiting room until I was called in. The room was big, with a huge, scary-looking machine in the middle.

At the side of the room was a glass partition with seats behind it. Mum was asked to sit behind the glass, so she could still see me but not be exposed to unnecessary radiation. I was asked to step up into the machine and stand in front of a secondary machine. They gave me a cup of this white chalky stuff; it tasted just as it looked, like chalk.

The lady who was in charge of the machine explained that they would be filming me swallowing and what happened next. She moved behind the glass partition and asked me to take a big gulp, which I did. The machines all started whirling. There was a screen attached to the machine, and I was able to see what the health care professional saw.

I watched my gulp go down my oesophagus (food tube) and into my stomach. After about 5 minutes of filming, we then watched the radioactive glow go back up the oesophagus, on the screen, and I vomited it out.

From my understanding, they were very happy with this. I was invited to step out of the machine, and I got changed back into my school uniform. We said goodbye to the nice lady and headed out for food. Mum seldom took us to fast food restaurants, but after the test, she took me to Burger King, which was on the hospital site, *healthy!*

I got a kiddie's meal with nuggets, and this felt like such a treat. We then went to drive home. I was excited to get home and watch TV and get into my pyjamas, as this would be the cherry on the cake—TV time, and I wasn't even sick. Plus, this was all before school finished.

As we started driving home, this awful noise came from under the car. Mum looked at where the noise was coming from, and she told me that our exhaust had fallen off. We drove very slowly to the closest mechanics, where I sat on a plastic green chair, whilst they fixed it.

I had never been to a mechanic's before and was so excited to have a nosey. But after one hour playing with my Burger King toy, I got bored. By the third hour, I was very bored, and the excitement of leaving school early was a distant dream.

A few weeks later, I got to leave school early again for the doctor's appointment. The nice doctor in a white coat looked at me over her big table. She had hazel eyes, which were kind. She explained that my oesophageal sphincter, or the muscle at the end of my food pipe, does not work properly and allows stomach contents back into my mouth.

She informed us that I had gastro-oesophageal reflux disease (known as GERD/GORD or reflux) and a sliding hernia (or hiatus hernia). In this, a part of one's stomach slides up, causing pressure in the stomach, pushing food into the oesophagus.

The doctor advised me to continue the medication, just have more of it, as I was now bigger, and then discharged me, and life continued as it was, until the admission.

* * * *

We now return to a lovely Wednesday evening, in October 2004, aged 11 years old. Mum picked Sarah and me up in our silver Zafira from my auntie's house, where my cousins and I had been watching TV after school. The sun was setting over the hill, producing an orange and pink sky, as we drove the 5 minutes to our house.

My sister was sitting in the back of the car, chatting about her day in primary school. Mum and I listened intently. I rested my head on the glass window as I watched the houses pass us by and nodded off.

Now that I had moved up to secondary school, it was nice hearing about the excitement of my old primary, but all this high school malarkey was exhausting. When we got home, I ran upstairs to take off my brown uniform to my floordrobe and got into my PJs. Then I plonked myself on my bed and starfished. I was so exhausted.

I was obviously aware that I was exhausted, but it was difficult to tell whether the exhaustion stemmed from getting over the bronchitis and returning to school or the lack of nutrition due to the vomiting. I was completely oblivious to the significance of the symptoms.

Mum, however, had noticed. She had also noticed my pale skin, dry lips, looser clothes and sweet breath (when you lose weight, you produce ketones, which could alter your breath smell apparently).

The following day after school, Mum took me to A&E.

I had been to A&E lots of times over the years, for injuries, sprains and breaks, but never, to my memory, because I was ill (I don't remember the meningitis). Mum and I sat in the waiting room, which was painted yellow and blue; most likely to make the place look friendlier and calmer.

The waiting room was filled with toys for the younger kids. The waiting room had a chemical smell, mixed with cleaning solution. I rested my head on my mum's shoulder as I was called through by a nurse.

Initially, they took my blood pressure and put a clip on my finger to check my pulse rate and oxygen levels. They then took my blood and they poked a little tube, a cannula, into the back of my hand. The nurse explained that I was dehydrated and that I would need fluid to hydrate myself. They then connected fluids to the cannula.

All these new things were a little intimidating, but Mum seemed content with what was happening, and so I just went with it. I was called into a room where a doctor, who was in his late 20s, with brown eyes and brown short hair was sitting. He asked me to lie on the bed, which was also in the room.

He pressed on my stomach and asked Mum and me questions. I remember being too nervous to answer them. He explained that I would have an ultrasound and then be admitted to the ward.

He left quickly after confirming that we had no more questions, and we were left alone in this room. We sat there in silence. The A&E was such an array of noises and smells, it felt a bit overwhelming, but Mum was with me, so I was okay.

After what seemed like ages, a porter came with a wheelchair and I was taken to an ultrasound. I was wheeled through the adult A&E, which had become a buzz with activity. We went down the now-empty halls of the hospital—as the 9–5 workers had gone home—to ultrasound.

Sitting in the ultrasound waiting room, on one side, there were two people in beds: one was hooked up to tubes and bags, which were coming out of different parts of her, and the other gentleman was distressed, rolling about in their bed, crying out. The health care worker with them tried to settle him.

I felt a little scared by this and held onto my mum's hand a little tighter.

We did not wait long before we were taken into yet another room. A man sat behind a computer, which was next to a bed, on which he asked me to lie. He pulled my top up to expose my abdomen and then told me he would be placing gel onto my stomach.

Within seconds, he had done this and then placed a scanning probe on it. I felt very uncomfortable and exposed, but Mum was there, so I knew this was okay. I even tried to move the tissue paper that I was lying on to cover myself a little bit more.

The man then asked me about my periods, and I blushed with embarrassment. We were not a period-positive family, and we did not talk about periods. Because of the way we were brought up, I believed them to be something that people did not talk about.

So, when he asked me, in front of my mum, I was shocked and wanted the ground to eat me up. Not to mention that he was a man, which doubled down on the embarrassment. I managed to mumble some form of response, and he seemed to be happy with what he heard.

After around 10 minutes of moving the probe across my abdomen, he told me that he had finished. He handed me the tissue paper I was lying on, which was some of the hardest tissue paper I had ever felt, to wipe the gel away. I left the ultrasound room and sat back on the wheelchair, then the porter appeared from thin air, pushed the wheelchair to the ward.

* * * *

The ward was dark, as by now it was night. We were taken into a bay, where all the curtains but one were drawn. I could hear a baby cry in the distance and mumbling behind the curtains. We were wheeled to the curtained area that was not closed, and a nurse appeared from behind us.

She introduced herself and asked me to get onto the bed, helping me with my fluid bag. The porter said his goodbyes and went out the same way we arrived. The nurse helped pull out a camp bed for Mum, then sat on it, next to Mum, to ask some booking questions, like: what school do you go to? And what is your religion?

She then advised us to try and sleep, but if we needed anything, there was a button to press, and she handed me the nurse call bell. She then took my blood pressure and said good night, leaving us.

Mum and I looked at each other, and she then passed me pyjamas, which I got into. Mum had brought a just-in-case bag full of essentials. I felt a little nervous but also a little excited, like this was a little adventure of new experiences.

I lay back onto my bed thinking of everything I had just experienced and seen. I soon heard the gentle purr of Mum's snore, before I dropped off to sleep too.

When I woke up in the morning, I looked at Mum, who was still asleep. The drip in my hand was still going, and I looked around at the curtains, which had animals on them. I then looked to the ceiling, which had pictures drawn and painted on by patients. I wondered if I could do this today? I was filled with nervous anticipation.

As the ward became noisier, Mum woke up and started fussing. I got washed and clothed. The doctors came around explaining that I would have more tests and that I would be staying on the fluids. After the doctor's round, Mum went home for a few hours to get clean clothes.

The ward had a school room, and after the ward's round, the teacher came around and asked me about school. I was taken to the school room where they would teach for three hours, a mixture of English, math, science and history. They said they would contact my school, so I would not miss out on anything, which was a relief.

In the afternoon, the play specialist came around and showed me the playroom, which happened to be right by my bed. She explained that she would do activities with me, to pass the time, sometimes arts and crafts or maybe other fun activities, in-between all the hospital bits and bobs.

Just like the doctors said, over the next few days, I underwent investigations. The first test was a repeat ultrasound. During this investigation, they found that I had a duplex kidney; two tubes coming from my kidney, but only one going into my bladder.

Something that had not been picked up in the previous ultrasound, this would have no impact on my vomiting, though.

The next test I had was a barium swallow. This was the test I had way back when I was 7. Again, they stood me in front of a machine, gave me an awful-tasting chalky drink and waited for me to vomit. The thing is, I could not vomit on demand. They did not wait long before they sent me back to the ward.

However, once back at the ward, I vomited everything back up. Apparently, because they didn't capture the vomit, the result was normal.

The third test was where they gave me a radioactive scrambled egg to eat. I was not a fan of scrambled eggs at the time. Once I had eaten it, I was scanned to make sure it was in my stomach, and it was. I was asked to come back in an hour, where they would scan me again, as it should have started being digested and in the top part of the bowel.

In that hour, I went back up to the ward, where on the way, I vomited up all the egg. When I was scanned an hour later, the egg was no longer in my stomach. Apparently, because it was no longer in my stomach, this meant my digestion was normal.

I did not really understand why I needed all these investigations. I just went along with what the doctors wanted. I had reflux, I knew that, and my parents knew that. Why did the doctors not understand that?

* * * *

Each day was the same; get up, get washed and dressed, the doctor's round, Mum leaves, school time, hospital tests, play therapist, Dad's visits, wash, PJs, Mum and bed, and throughout all this, I would be having fluids.

The doctors occasionally changed my medication, and I just went along with it. However, one day became two, four, three weeks, and I was still on the ward, taking everything in my stride.

Dad was now undertaking all Mum's jobs at home, including looking after Sarah, getting her up, getting her dressed, taking her to school and putting her to bed. As well as cooking and cleaning. We had support from other mums in the school playground and my wonderful auntie, who also picked her up from school regularly.

Dad was a little bit like a fish out of water, and found some of these jobs difficult, as they were Mum's job, but he had to learn fast and be on his feet. Sarah recalled a story where he took Sarah to school one morning, and one of the mums had to redo Sarah's hair, as what our dad did was bad.

It hurt my heart to think that Dad and Sarah were left to fend for themselves over this period of time, especially Sarah, who was banded about between family and friends for childcare reasons.

I have always felt guilty about this, and I hope she knew that if I could change it, I would have, but I was also aware that it was not my fault and was completely out of my control. Mum and Dad were just trying their best and were having to parent reactively to the situation.

* * * *

Each day on the ward, there were new patients.

The appendicitis kids would be taken in, not eating or nil by mouth, as it was called. Dressed in a gown and whisked to the theatre. If their appendix had not exploded, they would be on the ward for a day or two. If their appendix had exploded or ruptured, as they called it, they would be in there a week before they could go home.

Children with broken bones would be in and out, one day following surgery and would have exciting stories of how they injured themselves, usually it involved trampolines.

One kid had been hit by a car and got into the local paper; he was there for two weeks. He was the VIP of the ward.

Then there were the diarrhoea twins. Who were unluckily put in the same bay as me. They were around 8 months of age, and if one was not crying, the other was. They constantly had family and extended family around them—overnight, too.

I thought the family forgot they were not the only people in the bay, as every time one of the children had a bowel explosion, the commotion that followed was something that would mirror the frontline in wartime. Due to the nature of their disease, this would happen often—too often. The smell that came with it could make hardened criminals cry.

* * * *

It was week four when the doctors spoke to Mum and me during the doctor's round, explaining they were concerned about the weight loss and that I needed regular IV fluid to stay hydrated. They explained that I could have a nasogastric tube, or an NG tube—as it's known—inserted.

This tube would go into my nose and down into my stomach. They would use it to administer medication and nutrition. This may help me tolerate my medication and also give me nutrients.

Mum spoke to the doctors about how worried she was about my nutrition and weight loss, and she welcomed this step.

Hearing Mum speak about how worried she was made me feel very guilty. Even though I had no control over my health, I was still putting her through it, so I agreed to the tube, but in truth, I had very little understanding of what this meant.

Later that same day, I was taken to the procedures room with a nurse and a student nurse. The procedure room was a small room towards the left of the entrance of the ward. They used it to keep all their utilities, but there was a medical couch in the middle of the room, where one would undergo procedures. It was a very bright room, and it smelled very, very medical.

Over the past four weeks, I got to know this nurse, and she was very nice. She told me not to worry and asked me to lie on the couch. She measured the tube against the side of my face and the middle of my chest. She dipped the end of the tube in lubricant jelly and proceeded to push it up my nostril.

It felt a little bit like them COVID swabs that tickled your brain, but worse.

As it hit the bridge of my nose, it was extremely uncomfortable, but it was not painful. It poked around the back of my nostril before going down the back of my throat, at which point the nurse told me to swallow.

She offered me some water, but decided not to give me the water because if I vomited, I would vomit up the tube, so she advised me to dry swallow, which I did. After pushing it down, she secured the tube against my cheek and got a syringe and pulled back on the tube with the syringe.

With the fluid that came out, she went and tested it on pH paper. She was happy with the result. (They do this test to confirm they have acid from your stomach, to make sure it's not in your lungs.)

If I was honest, I didn't think much of the tube. I didn't see it as a long-term solution or something to worry about, just something temporary that would go once the vomiting calmed down. That was my understanding of it. Although it was uncomfortable.

The dietitians came and set up a feeding plan. I would have to be fed overnight and then three boluses throughout the day, and we started. I didn't feel sick. I wasn't in pain. I continued to vomit, though, which included the feed too. The tube wasn't really a problem. I'd prefer to eat, but that was not working for me at the moment. I managed.

The following Tuesday, a lady in a purple top came in to show us how to use the feeding pump. That wasn't rocket science; it was fairly easy to use, and I was excited that they felt I was important enough and old enough to teach me how to use the machine. It gave me a little bit of control back.

Mum seemed okay with this too; she was pragmatic, absorbing all the information the lady who was training us was giving. Although to help her remember, she did write a little cheat sheet.

That Wednesday morning, the doctors came around for the doctor's ward round and told me that I would be going home. They confirmed that they would give me some feed to cover the next two days, and I would receive a feed delivery, and that was that. They said it so blasé, as though they were always sending children home with tubes.

In the four weeks I had been in the hospital, every single child had gone home better than when they were admitted. Why not me? My heart sank to my feet. I could not comprehend what they just said. I have a tube now. I couldn't go home with it. I need to be better. Hospitals make you better. I was leaving the hospital worse than when I came in. I'm not fixed.

What it did mean was that they had not found any significant causes for my vomiting or anything of concern. What it did mean was that the medications were no longer working on me to manage my condition. What it did mean was that I was on long-term nutrition, and this was going to be a long-term issue.

I remember leaving the hospital feeling really confused. I was confused as to why I hadn't been fixed, because that was what happens in hospitals, and I was confused as to why Mum agreed to me having the tube at home. I had never met anybody with a tube before.

I'd never even met anybody with reflux before. I felt completely alone and isolated. Could I go to school with it? What does my future hold? Everything ran through my brain on that journey home. I was so tired it felt like my brain was going to implode.

However, I was also really excited to sleep in my bed, to annoy my sister and to be a family again.

Looking back, this was the moment my identity changed from healthy to disabled. The world turned on its head, and I just had to react to it. I don't think I comprehended the significance of this moment, but on reflection, I do now.

I wish that at this point I had been provided counselling for dealing with life-changing conditions. As an adult, I am aware they have started linking mental health services with chronic illness, but they just didn't back then.

* * * *

My first night home, my mum didn't connect my feed, not because we wanted to go against the hospital, but we just wanted a moment of normal.

'We will start properly tomorrow,' she said, 'but for tonight, we will be normal.'

I climbed up onto my bunk bed and curled up in a ball, and I remember crying—really crying. I didn't understand what was happening. I cried myself to sleep that night, the first night of many.

Years before, when we were choosing rooms, I'm not sure how, but Sarah had managed to get the bigger room, and I had the small room with the bunk bed. Unfortunately, bunk beds were not conducive to night-time feeds or disability.

So, Dad took my mattress from my bunk bed and placed it on the floor of Sarah's bedroom the following day. Sarah and I would now share a room with a plan for the future, of Sarah moving to the small room.

Not only had Sarah's world been turned upside down, with Dad becoming Sarah's primary carer, with her having to share Mum between me and the hospital, and worrying about her older sister. But she also lost her bedroom and the privacy that came with it.

Being home was lovely, though. I had my floor bed, which was still more comfortable than the hospital beds. I had my duvet and pillow too, which felt and smelled like home. The bedroom did look a little like a hospital with giving sets and feeding and machines, but it was home.

Mum and Dad tried to make life as normal as possible. I got to watch TV with Sarah under the duvet. I got to argue with Sarah, because, well, we were sisters. I got to bathe in my own bath. I know I was only in the hospital for 1 month, but that's a long time when you are a child.

With this happiness that came with being home came a sadness. I truly did not understand what was happening. I went in as a person with reflux, and I came out disabled. Life, as we knew it, had changed.

* * * *

To manage the fact, I was refluxing so often, I started carrying around a vomit jug. Every time I refluxed, I would fill it up, and when it was full, I would flush it down the toilet. I would vomit food, drink, feed and just pure acid.

My teeth felt too sensitive to brush, and my breath smelled bad. Every time my parents saw the full vomit jug, I could see the sadness in their eyes, like I was chipping away at their hearts.

On the rare occasion, I went out, with this tube across my face, I was tarnished as a sick person, like it was a branding and now my identity. People would stare at me, take in my face and then they would give sympathetic eyes to my mum.

It's an experience all visibly disabled people experience; if you know, you know.

One lady in the pet shop grabbed my mum by her arm and outright asked her, 'Why does she have a tube up her nose?'

As though it was her birthright to know.

Whilst at home, I got into a routine. Mum would wake me up, I would go downstairs and sit in front of the mind-numbing TV. Old casualty, old bill, doctors, diagnosis murder, really wild show, crocodile hunter and Sue Thomas FBI, before Sarah, Mum and Dad came home.

They would eat, and I would go to bed. I did this every day at home, and soon the days merged into one. I would only know it was the weekend when there was no argument in the morning from Mum trying to get Sarah up—she loved sleeping.

The only time my routine changed was with hospital appointments, if my tube got dislodged and on Wednesdays when my grandma came. Grandma would try to get me up and about. I just could not really see what the point was. I was sick, and no one cared to fix me; they just gave me a tube and told me to get on with it.

Looking back now. Grandma tried her best, and for years, I felt guilty for not making an effort. All the time she wasted trying to get me to participate in life, and I just wanted to curl up in a ball. She died when I was 16, and my heart shattered into a billion pieces, because I knew I was never going to get this time back. I could never say sorry.

Over the years, I have come to realise, this was the start of depression. A depression that was never acknowledged or addressed in reaction to my situation. Grandma did not understand, and no one else was there. The only constant was TV and Sims. I had control of that. That was my world.

The hospital visits were regular, a few times a week, because I was vomiting so often that the NG tube would dislodge and the tip would come out of my mouth. The first time this happened was terrifying. I was having a jam doughnut in the bath *because I'm classy,* and I went to vomit, and the tube tip came out of my mouth.

I wrapped a towel around me and ran downstairs to show Mum. She called the hospital, and we were told to come up to the ward for the tube to be replaced. The nurse told us that if it happened again, to just pull the tube out, and then come, instead of travelling with the tube going in my nose and out of my mouth.

The next time we pulled it out. The only exception was the time that the tube got caught on the ridge of my nose, and the pain was so intense. I spent the 30-minute drive trying to stay as still as possible, because a single shift caused shooting pain in my face. The nurse just gave it a strong yank, and it came out before she re-sited it.

I have made it sound like I was out of the hospital for months; it was only weeks. As I was still vomiting, I was still getting dehydrated, and I was readmitted. Mum had been off work looking after me, and I became her full-time job.

Dad was working, and the village, consisting of family, school and church friends, was looking after Sarah. I would be admitted, hydrated, and discharged. The more it happened, the more difficult it was for me to go in, as it became clear that the hospital was not looking for any fix or cure. The more I was discharged, the more it was cemented that this was it.

Eating became harder and harder. I once had been the girl who would ask for seconds and thirds of dinner. Who would eat anything and everything (except shellfish after a horrific food poisoning incident aged 7). But now, food was no longer fun or tasty. I looked for food that tasted okay when vomiting.

I would look for food that would be easy to vomit up to stop me from choking. The hospital kept telling me that if I stopped vomiting, this would stop the tube from coming up. I knew that by stopping vomiting, it would stop my parents' unhappiness and it would let Sarah and me return to our normal lives.

The logic being if I stopped eating, then I would vomit less, making everyone happy.

* * * *

I was readmitted with dehydration in November. One morning, during the ward round, the consultant informed Mum that she had sat in training with the *gut club*. She explained that she had been networking with a paediatric gastrointestinal consultant who was based at a different local hospital, St Alice's, and my situation came up.

After talking through my case, this gastrointestinal consultant called Dr Zhang, was going to organise more tests on the 25 November 2004, for what the doctors were calling an endoscopy. All I knew was that I could not eat from midnight and that I would be asleep.

This gave me so much hope, I did not care how awful the tests were going to be; they were going to find out what caused my reflux to worsen and cure me.

On the night of 24 November, a friend from school came to visit me out of the blue. She had gone to my primary school and was in my form at secondary school. She brought a card signed by everyone in my form, and it was so nice to see that the other students, some of whom I had only been with for three weeks, had not forgotten me.

Each message wished me well, some gave me their MSN handles, *because I am that old*, and some told me school was boring. We went through the messages together whilst sharing chips from the canteen. As we munched away, she told me all the gossip. Each story was like literature to my ears.

I had not been around anyone of my age for 2.5 months by now and loved hearing all the stories and news. By the end of visiting time, I was fully caught up, and my mind was completely off the procedure tomorrow. I got ready for bed, vomited and fell asleep.

I still have the cards my school friends sent to me in a memory box. I couldn't begin to explain what it meant to me. It made me feel missed and loved, which was exactly what I needed.

On the morning of the endoscopy, Mum drove me to St Alice's Hospital. It was only in the next town over, and the drive was not very long, roughly 30 minutes. As I got out of the car, in the car park, I looked over to this vast building.

Where it was once white, it was now grey, and paint was peeling off the exterior walls. Mum and I navigated through the maze that was the corridors of this hospital and found ourselves in the children's hospital.

The hospital I had been admitted to when I was a child had closed down and moved to this hospital, where it had been reopened. However, like many NHS hospitals, money was tight, and you could see in its ageing appearance that it had seen better days.

The inside of the hospital was painted with the same colour as the outside of the hospital, and just like the exterior, the interior was also peeling from the walls. The hospital also smelt like a hospital, a mixture of cleaning products and sterilisation products.

We went to the fourth floor of the children's hospital, which was the day surgery unit. Unlike the main hospital, the adult hospital, the children's floors were painted with bright colours, although ageing, and seemed to be friendlier and happier.

A kindly nurse greeted us and confirmed my name. She then brought me to the waiting room, which was filled with children's toys and had a portable TV in the middle, although it did not work. The ward smelled different to the main hospital, like what I later learnt was anaesthetic gas.

Mum and I sat in the playroom until a gentleman who looked around, 50, came into the room. He was Malaysian, with hazelnut eyes that peered over his glasses in an intelligent-looking way. He wore a white coat, like the doctors on TV.

He introduced himself as Dr Zhang, and my mum sat up straight and appeared to experience a mixture of excitement and relief to see him. He was the specialist gastrointestinal paediatric that North Surrey Hospital had talked to.

To Mum and me, he was going to be the miracle man who was going to cure me. Little did we know this was going to be the start of a long and interesting therapeutic relationship.

'Hello, Kayleigh, I heard you have been causing problems at North Surrey,' he said with a smile. 'Hopefully, we'll be able to work out what's happening today. I will be doing your procedure. I just need your Mum to sign this consent form.'

Dr Zhang explained to me what he was doing: placing a camera into my stomach, via my mouth, and taking some samples. He went through the terms and conditions, the side effects, the possible injuries, and Mum signed my life away. He asked if I had any questions, and I shook my head. Mum confirmed it by saying, 'No, I think you've answered everything I would have asked.'

With that, he left the room with one final look and a calming smile before shutting the door behind him. I watched him walk down the hall through the windows till I could no longer see him.

Then I looked at Mum, who looked nervous, but also positive with anticipation, as though this would be the answer; this test would show something and would answer all our prayers.

I remember being so nervous that I had chewed and spit my nails to shreds. I was chewing my last nail when the nurse came in a gulp. She handed me a gown to get into, which I quickly put on. The nurse, Mum and I walked along the hall and entered an area that had big signs saying *staff only*.

We walked a little bit further, turning left through double doors, and I entered a much smaller room. There were two people in this room wearing scrubs and masks. I was ushered onto the bed, where I lay down. It smelt even more like anaesthetic gas. Everybody introduced themselves. They seemed kind, and nobody was very worried or anxious.

This soothed me a little bit, but I continued to be very nervous. Dr Zhang poked his head through the door. He was no longer wearing his white coat and had changed into blue scrubs. He also seemed calm, and this helped.

One of the doctors used the cannula that I already had placed at North Surrey and started pushing thick white liquid into it. I remember it stung so much, and I started crying out and trying to fight it—but there was no hope. Everything went black.

The next thing I knew, I was in a different room. I could feel the breeze on my face. My throat was sore and dry. Without opening my eyes, I tried to itch my nose, but was stopped by a mask on my face. I slowly opened my eyes to see Mum holding my hand, whilst sitting down next to me.

As she had seen me move, she had gotten up and was peering over the side of my bed at me. She told me how well I had done and that it was okay if I was feeling a little woozy.

Everything looked hazy, but as I blinked multiple times, things started becoming a bit more solid. As I slowly woke up more, they removed my oxygen and brought me to the main ward.

On the main ward, there were four beds in the bay. At the top of each bed, on the wall, there was a different Disney character. Although, just like the rest of the hospital, it had aged and was chipping. The nurse came in and told me I would be feeling funny for probably a few hours, but that when I was ready, I could get up and dress.

As I hated wearing the gown, I did that straight away, and yes, I did feel wobbly and my head was a bit spinny, but I powered through and got back into my clothes.

Dr Zhang came to my bedside before I was discharged. He greeted Mum and me again and confirmed that the procedure had gone well. He went on to inform us that the top of my bowel was inflamed (duodenitis), my stomach was inflamed (gastritis); as well as my oesophagus (oesophagitis). He explained that he was going to recommend new medications.

He turned to leave and then stopped, turned back around and said, 'Kayleigh, could I ask you…when did you have chips?'

'Oh, last night, and I vomited some,' I replied, bemused.

'Ahh, okay,' he said with a smile, 'because they were still present in your stomach—undigested.'

By his and Mum's reaction, this was not normal. But I could not quite gauge how abnormal this was.

It turned out that it should have been digested in 4 hours and that they should not have been sitting in my stomach 21 hours later, undigested.

'And Kayleigh,' he continued, 'when did you eat the finger nail?'

My cheeks went bright red. 'OH…just before I went in.'

'Kayleigh, why did you not spit it out?' Mum interjected, bemused.

I turned to her and said, 'Because they had called me in, and I panicked!'

Dr Zhang chuckled and said that this was a first for him. Mum laughed and seemed fairly satisfied with this response. I wanted the ground to swallow me whole.

Dr Zhang then said his goodbyes and left.

I was driven back to the other hospital by my mum. The car journey back felt very short; there was so much to unpack. I had a diagnosis. Would the new medication cure me?

Back on the ward, I got into my pyjamas and was reconnected to the fluids, and I went to sleep, with Mum on the camp bed next to me. She snored that night, and although I hated the fact she snored, it felt like this was the first night in a long time that she slept deeply enough to snore.

* * * *

The following morning, as per usual, I got up, got dressed and waited for the doctors to come around with Mum. They were happy with the change of medication and agreed that all this inflammation was caused by my reflux and a hiatus hernia.

This was the first time in the past three months that something had seemed positive. I was excited to try the new medication because then I could get better and go back to school. I had seen that everyone missed me from the letters they had sent. I wanted to feel normal again. I wanted everything to return to our usual. I had hope!

The plan was that I would be discharged from the hospital today, 3 December, after starting the new medication. Whilst I was waiting for the medication from the pharmacy, I was able to watch the health care staff put the Christmas decorations up on the ward. The joy and happiness that the decorations brought made me feel all Christmassy inside.

I am an autumn/winter person. I absolutely love Christmas and the lead-up to Christmas. Putting up the decorations, watching vomit-inducing cringy Christmas movies, oversized jumpers, as well as the stormy weather, the rain and being cosy. It's just my favourite time of year.

Over the next few days, I waited patiently for the vomiting to improve. I was taking the medication. I was doing what the doctors said to the letter. I was on my feed every night. I was having the three boluses a day, and I was waiting—just waiting.

I thought Mum wanted us to get our minds off the fact that we were waiting for the medication to work, so that weekend we put up our Christmas decorations. Mum and Dad opened up the attic where our Christmas things live.

We had the annual argument over the state of the attic. The four of us dragged the tree and ornaments in bits and pieces, down the stairs and into the front room.

Our front room was Mum's good room; we only ever used it for events or when people came to our house. However, our front room came into its own around Christmas time. It had green carpeted floors, with cream walls and a red sofa.

Colours that were an ode to County Mayo, which was the county in Ireland that my maternal grandparents were from, I was convinced this was why Mum chose these colours.

So, when Christmas came around, it was the perfect deluxe Christmas colour chart. Our Christmas tree, which sat in the corner of the room, was decorated with red and gold baubles, as well as wooden ornaments and homemade arts and crafts that had built up over the years.

My paternal grandparents' last Christmas card to us was placed centre stage, on our mantelpiece. There was a light arch that sat on our windowsill, visible from the outside, and we had a little manger scene, which sat comfortably in a cove of the room, which we sometimes decorated.

One Christmas when I was 7, Sarah and I used the nativity scene as a house, and brought down our Barbies, Brats dolls (I had Barbies; Sarah preferred Brats), plus used the ornaments from the Christmas tree as well as the nativity scene figurines—to play house and make a little community.

Mum thought it was so funny that sporty Barbie was Mum to baby Jesus. She took a photo and remind us every year.

We removed the layer of dust on the tree box from where it sat dormant for the year in the attic. We put Christmas music on the stereo and started putting our home-Christmas-scene together, just like we do every year, a mirror image.

And just like every year, Sarah disappeared to have a three-hour bath, whilst I decorated the tree with Mum. Sarah would then come back downstairs and take all the credit. It was a nice little bit of normality.

The next few days, Mum and Dad tried to keep life as normal as possible. Sarah was finishing school for the winter and was getting excited about all the sleeping and eating she would be doing over Christmas. However, our lives continued to be splattered with hospital appointments, vomit and hospital visits, especially when I vomited the tube out.

Multiple times a week. The vomiting just didn't get better, and each day, my heart hurt just a little bit more. I was also under the care of the district nurses; they were called out twice when my tube got blocked. Which they fixed with Coke of all things.

I remember trying to keep myself cheerful and occupied on Christmas, but anytime I was by myself, my brain would become sad.

* * * *

In the Catholic faith, Christmas and Easter are the high points of the religious calendar. Up to the point I had been in the hospital, I had been an altar server at our church. Christmas and Easter were an altar server's bread and butter.

There would be lots of additional masses and extra services that had additional jobs to undertake, and we would usually be rewarded with chocolate on Christmas Day to say thanks. I enjoyed being an altar server; it made the mass go quicker as we were constantly doing things.

As Christmas was coming up, I asked Mum if I could go back to my altar-serving duties whilst I was out of the hospital. We needed to put our names on a list as some of the training was coming up, and although I pretty much knew what to do, because it didn't really change year on year.

However, the training meant that I could undertake the duties and all the masses I would be forced to go to would be bearable, as I was busy (I was a tween after all and church was not my scene anymore). Also, this was me trying to be normal, something that I hadn't felt in a long time. Mum thought about it for a little bit, just a few seconds, and she shook her head.

'No, Kayleigh, not this year. We don't want to look like you're trying to show the tube on your face. You'd be better sitting at the back of the choir. You can help the choir with their songs.'

I didn't argue. I just accepted what she said. Although I wasn't particularly trying to show off the tube. It showed itself off without me needing to do anything. I wanted things to get back to normal, and this felt normal for me. But I understood what my mum was saying.

As an adult, I reflect on this moment a lot, because there was a sense of ableism to it, a sense of hiding the disabled person away, and it doesn't sit right with me. I knew that was not what Mum was doing. I thought she was trying to protect me, but everyone was going to see the tube anyway, it didn't matter where I sat.

Easter and Christmas were a big thing for the choir as well. There were more masses and services, so more singing and music. My parents had a community in the church, where they attended every Sunday and would have a choir practice once a week.

Their fellow choir members became friends, and then friends became like family. So, when I first became sick, the people at church prayed for me and supported my parents, and my parents needed that support too. I always looked at it that any additional prayer couldn't hurt and was beneficial.

Because I was in the hospital around the time I had my diagnosis, I didn't get to see all the happiness and best wishes that came my way. Mum told me in the hospital how happy people were for me.

However, over the Christmas period, when things should have started improving and I was out of the hospital, I did see their faces when I informed them that things were not improving. I then saw the look of disappointment and sadness instead.

The look of disappointment made me feel like I was letting people down. It was as though I wasn't trying hard enough to get better. This feeling made me feel very alone, and I started not wanting people to know my bad news.

However, because Mum and Dad needed the support, they would attend church and talk to everyone. For me, going to church made me feel even more alone and isolated.

I had started to feel a little abandoned by God, too. It felt complicated. I had only been sick for four months, but these four months had turned everything upside down, and I wasn't getting any better, and I didn't understand why.

I didn't understand what I had done wrong to be punished, because this felt like a punishment. I couldn't work out why God didn't like me, as I had done everything right thus far. When I spoke to Mum and Dad, they told me that God sends us difficulties that he knows we could get through. So, I held on to this hope.

* * * *

Sarah finished off the school term, and the week before Christmas became a smorgasbord of Christmas shopping, gift wrapping, meeting up with friends, meeting up with family, and food shopping. Also, Christmas movies, Christmas Panto, Christmas music, Christmas jumpers, everything Christmas. My mum tried to fit it all in just to bring happiness to our faces.

Most importantly, in the days leading up to Christmas and Christmas Day, I was out of the hospital and at home!

Just like every year, Mum and Dad took us to the 6 pm mass, which was the children's mass full of music and singing. Dad went on to do the midnight mass music, which was normally started by a carol concert.

Mum and Dad would say that the midnight mass was too late for us to attend, even though we would try and stay up for when Dad came back at 01:00 am, because we were allowed to open one Christmas present.

On Christmas Day, I woke up super early and ran into Sarah's room, waking her up. The two of us then ran into Mum and Dad's room and got told to go back to bed for another hour or two, but Sarah and I were too excited and we spent the time playing in her room.

Mum and Dad eventually came into Sarah's room and said we could go downstairs. Just like every year, Dad would go down first to make sure Santa had come (for Sarah). He went into the front room, through the closed door, and put the Christmas music on.

Sarah and I crept down the stairs, waiting for Dad to say we could come in. We finally heard the special words and opened the door to see Christmas presents stuffed up the chimney and the Christmas tree with presents underneath it.

We spent the next hour as a family, opening up all our Christmas presents, enjoying every moment. We felt like a normal family. We hadn't experienced this feeling since I had gotten ill.

Dad then started stressing that he was going to be late with his preparation for Christmas Day Mass. Mum tried to calm him down, to no avail. Sarah and I were too busy playing with our gifts. *I couldn't quite remember what I got that year, but I would have loved it.*

We helped Mum tidy away all the discarded Christmas wrapping. Mum was just chucking it all away in the black bags, and me taking it out to work out what's for recycling. Sarah then had breakfast, whilst I had a bolus of feed. Sarah and I then got dressed and, just like every year, rushed to Christmas Day Mass, being late by a minute or two.

Having to sneak in at the back of the church when everyone stood up, and tiptoeing around the side of the congregation before they sat back down. *If you have never been to a Catholic mass, it involves a lot of standing sitting and kneeling.* Christmas Day Mass, like always, was filled with songs and wishing Merry Christmas to each other, and again, it was normal.

After mass, we went home and Mum started cooking the Christmas turkey with all the trimmings. The house smelled beautiful with the turkey roasting. Sarah and I set the table, extra Christmassy with crackers, and Mum let us use the posh cutlery as Christmas Day was special.

When the Christmas Day meal was ready, I only ate small portions of one or two mouthfuls of each item, partly because I was so worried that I would end up vomiting up the tube. The food melted in my mouth, though. I loved every moment of it. Just like every year, Mum brought a Christmas pudding, which she would put a £1 inside.

Mum and Dad attempted to set it on fire and then bickered over how to set it on fire. The fire itself was unimpressive, and then Mum cut the cake, giving me some. I reminded her, like I do every year, that I was not a fan and do not like raisins. Just like every year, Mum would say, but you had it last year, and I would remind her that I didn't.

Christmas afternoon, as a family of four, we drove over to our maternal cousin's house, where we shared presents with each other and wished each other a Merry Christmas. Mum and my auntie sat chatting in the kitchen with my cousin's other grandma, and my dad and uncle would sit in the lounge watching TV.

Sarah and I, our four cousins, caused chaos, running about the house playing Christmas games, until it started getting dark and Mum and Dad called Sarah and me to get back into the car. As our Christmas Day had not yet finished, we drove the hour to my grandparents' house.

We brought two plates full of our Christmas leftovers, for my grandparents, to their house. We never really exchanged presents, but we exchanged cards, and Grandma would normally have a second pudding for us to eat.

My dad seldom went to my grandparents' house, and when he did, my Grandad would always offer him a short of Irish whiskey, which my dad would always accept, as it would be rude not to. Also, because my dad had come, we sat in their smart room, the front room, and not the lounge where we would normally sit.

We stayed for about an hour and a half chatting all things Christmas before going back home and having leftovers before sitting in front of the TV. In our food comas, we watched whatever traumatic Christmas Day special played out on the TV before rolling ourselves into bed.

On Boxing Day, we got up early, as we drove an hour to Hampshire to visit my dad's sisters and brother. On Boxing Day, it was one of my cousin's birthdays too, and so it would be part Christmas, part birthday. This was usually done by opening presents in the evening, and at the Christmas meal, we would sing Happy Birthday to my cousin.

We really did try and separate Christmas from his birthday, but it was very much an amalgamation of Christmastime and birthday. In the evening, my cousins and I played dress up with my cousin's incredible chest of dressing up items, whilst my two other cousins, the boys, started play fighting. It was organised chaos, and I loved every moment of it.

We stayed at our cousin's house for one night. Every year, my cousins and I tried to stay up all night, watching ghost stories and failed. As we fell asleep to the adults laughing around an open fire. In the morning, my aunt put on a breakfast spread, and we went on a country walk before heading back home.

* * * *

The no man's land between Christmas and New Year was nothing to write home about. I ended up needing my tube to be reinserted, but other than that, we spent it as a family. Sarah and Mum braved the shops on Boxing Day for the Boxing Day sales.

Whereas Dad and I stayed home: he on his computer and I watching Christmas movies. Dad would come in at the end of the Christmas movie to watch its climax, because that was the best bit.

I kept on with the new medicines, kept with the feeds and kept with the vomiting. It was just relentless. The days amalgamated, and before we knew it, it was New Year's Eve.

Ever since I could remember, we had seen the new year in the hall connected to my parents' church, and this year would be no different. It was not a religious event, just a party where the congregation went to let their hair down. There was food, live music, and the party goers would dance the night in, with a countdown to midnight.

It was the first time I had really socialised since becoming unwell and with the tube. Most people at the church knew I was ill, as my name was under 'prayers for the sick' in the church newsletter.

Also, the tube gives it away, too. I got some sympathetic looks and was asked by another child if I had cancer. All in all, it was not awful and I had fun.

As the countdown started and midnight struck, I closed my eyes and wished that I would get better.

* * * *

Where most people were trying the new year, new me. For me, 2005 started with the new year, no change. In the days following the new year, I was admitted to the hospital with dehydration and vomiting.

My vomiting was not getting better, and I was losing weight as I was vomiting the tube feed and all the food I was eating.

I started seeing a dietitian, a skinny lady with straight brown hair. She was obsessed with me drinking milk and having yoghurts (which she pronounced Yooor gorts), and I could never take this seriously. She didn't seem to understand that it did not matter what I ate, I would vomit it up.

She started me on these build-you-up/give-you-calories shakes called Scandy shakes. I called them skanky-shakes because I was being a difficult teen.

I was being managed between the two hospitals. Dr Zhang looked after the gastric side, and North Surrey Hospital kept me alive. Dr Zhang was a breath of fresh air, he spoke about a surgery called a Nissen fundoplication.

They would use the top of my stomach or fundus (the technical name) and wrap it around the base of my oesophagus to strengthen the muscle that was not working well. A cure, maybe?

This was very exciting! We started feeling very positive. However, the surgery would be at a specialist hospital in London, and I would need more investigations before I could be referred.

On 18 January 2005, I was transferred to the Greengate Hospital, where I underwent evaluations. This hospital was designed so that if it failed, it could become a shopping mall, and it did have that look to it, with its white walls, blue floor.

Unlike my local hospital, the children's ward was much bigger and split into three sub-wards: one for teenagers, one for primary school age and the third was for babies. This ward also had an area which was a high dependency unit.

Each bay had six beds with blue curtains and a TV per bed for free, which was a luxury (although it turned off at 11).

Mum was not allowed to sleep next to me. Instead, there was a hospital relatives hotel where she stayed.

Whilst there, I underwent a variety of tests, like barium swallows, ultrasounds and X-rays.

Each day was similar to my local hospital, where I would get up, see the doctors for their rounds, and then take school/hospital tests. The school attached to the ward had more teachers and tech (computers), plus the room was much bigger.

On 24 January, I had another endoscopy under anaesthetic for photos and biopsies, where they took some cells from my stomach to test on. Similarly, to the last endoscopy, they put me under anaesthetic and I woke up with Mum next to me, holding my hand.

They had also made a plan which involved following the anaesthetic; they would try to switch me off and on again. They were to give me, to use the technical term, a fuck tone of IV anti-sickness to stop the sickness and slowly reduce it.

In the days following, the doctors came and told me the outcome of the endoscopy. It showed that even with all the medication I had been given, the inflammation in my stomach, duodenum and oesophagus had worsened. So, my medication was again amended. It also became clear that the reboot plan did not work either.

Yet more medications. I did not really understand why I needed all these tests. They had confirmed it was reflux, right? I just wanted everything to be back to normal.

I missed school. I missed home. I missed annoying my sister. I missed my bath and my own bed. I missed people not looking at me with pity. I hated vomiting; it was painful, smelly and messy. I missed eating without consequence, but I took it all in my stride.

In the hospital, everything was regimented: getting up, breakfast, doctor's rounds, school, lunch, visiting times, dinner, and going to bed. On top of that, everything was documented: eating, vomiting, drinking, IV fluids, urine, pooping…everything. I felt like a goldfish on display at all times.

The tests had become more invasive, sometimes painful and embarrassing. I was having strange men and women perform sometimes embarrassing exams on me. I was also having cannulas regularly, NG tubes. Each time was uncomfortable each time brought me a little bit more anxiety. I wanted to appear okay, but cracks had started to show.

Looking back now, I felt like I was the cause of everyone's problems. I felt guilty, not that I had much control over my symptoms, guilt that I was keeping mum from Sarah and Dad. I felt guilty that I was using up a hospital bed, I just had little old reflux. I felt like I was taking up space and that I was a hassle.

What I felt more though, was a longing to be normal again. The initial excitement of the first hospital admission was long gone. Instead, I was missing out on normal lives, and I felt it. With the hospital tests, I felt exposed, which was difficult as I was a private person and being asked if I had pooed that time today felt like too much information.

Each time the nurses and doctors came around would bring anxiety. What would they ask of me next, and whatever it would have been, I would have agreed to anything, no matter how embarrassing, because I wanted normal back.

One day, a lady with blonde hair tied back and flowy clothes came to my bedside. She told me she was a clinical psychologist. I was taken to a side room, and she asked me lots of questions. About life, about family and friends and about the vomiting. My mum was a mental health nurse, so I almost automatically trusted her more.

I opened up about how I was feeling and was honest. I remember just saying I don't think about vomiting, it just comes up.

I remember she asked me, 'Is it worse when you're stressed?'

I said yes.

I was told to tell the truth, stress did make it worse, but so did coughing, tight clothing, spicy food, being in water, yet she didn't ask about that. In the days following, things changed, but I did not think much of it until I returned to North Surrey Hospital. I just wanted the surgery so everything would get back to normal.

We returned to North Surrey Hospital on Thursday. Mum and Dad were told of a meeting they were asked to attend on the Friday. I asked to go because it was about me, but they said I was not allowed. So, at 03:00 pm on Friday, Mum and Dad came to the ward. Dad had to take time off work, so I knew it was important.

Mum told me afterwards that the consultant at North Surrey Hospital told my parents that they believed I was mentally ill, and this was now confirmed by the clinical psychologist, whom I had seen at Greengate.

They set forward a plan regarding my treatment and, in no uncertain terms, informed my parents that if they did not agree, they would look at taking steps to remove me from their care.

They informed my parents that there would be no surgery. I was referred to a community psychiatric nurse (CPN) and a psychiatrist, who were also present at the meeting, and that would be that.

Mum came out of that meeting and came over to me. The second I saw her face, I knew something was wrong. She tried to explain that they believed I was mentally ill, but that Mum and Dad knew that I wasn't. She went on to explain that we had to let things happen, to prove to them I wasn't. The world as I knew it changed.

That feeling of a mat being pulled from underneath me, like an earthquake when all the buildings around you fall down. I didn't understand. Me? Mentally ill. No, I was sad because I was sick, but I never caused myself to be sick. I didn't want to be sick any more. I wasn't choosing this life. I wanted to be normal. I didn't understand.

The ward made a plan. The consultant told me the plan on Monday morning during the ward round. I would be walked to the food trolley, supported in picking a healthy plate. Walked back to my bed, and I would be watched when eating and after eating, to stop me from vomiting. I would not be allowed to skip a meal.

She then said that if I refused, they had ways of making me eat without my permission, but they did not want to do that. Either way, I had no choice. They would do everything in their physical capability to not remind me to vomit.

Once my vomiting had reduced, I would be able to go home and back to school even with my tube. I would continue to receive mental health care. That was that. I had no say.

Mum and Dad agreed; they had no choice. It was better to agree, stay a part of something and have a say. Then to not have any say at all.

So, it began. I would be woken up to have breakfast. I would be taken to the trolley to pick out food. Someone would sit next to me when I ate it. The thing with reflux is, it's not normally a big vomit, it's lots of little mouthfuls of vomit. *TMI—I know.*

But food would get to my stomach, and in-between swallows, food would sometimes reflux, but in most cases, it would be after eating. This could be five minutes after eating, or it could be the day after.

However, this meant I could eat, vomit, and then continue eating. I had been doing this all of my life and was nonplussed by this. Most of the time, I vomited after food, but I had no control over when it happened; it just came when it wanted to.

I used to be a breakfast/morning person, but this had changed since I had been sick. I was no longer a breakfast or morning person. I found mornings hard as my sleep was affected by the vomiting. This particular morning, I had been woken up by one of the nurses, advising that I could choose between toast and cereal.

I struggle with bread, so I chose a cereal. I was given it by the housekeeper. I sat in the chair next to my bed, whilst still being half asleep. This morning, one of the health care assistants (HCAs) was tasked with observing me.

She was a bigger lady, with wonky teeth and short grey hair. I took one mouthful…then a second mouthful…then a third and a fourth mouthful. But I could start to feel the food coming up my food tube.

I had no control over it. I needed to be sick, and I looked around frantically for a vomit bowl, but there were none. They were not above the sink, which is where they normally were. There were none by the side of my bed. The ones that were there had been removed overnight.

My mouth was now full of vomit, I acted vomit bowl to the HCA, and she pretended she didn't see me, but I could feel another mouthful of vomit coming up. My mouth was full, I was going to choke if I didn't let this mouthful out, I opened my mouth, put my hands out and vomited over myself.

I was distraught. the last time I vomited over myself was when I was 4, and I was now a preteen. I had Cheerios and milk in my hands, down my top, in my cereal bowl.

I looked up at the HCA, and all she said was, 'Well, if you didn't vomit, you would not be in this situation.'

Tears came to my eyes as she stood up and walked out. Milk dripped off my fingers as I walked to the sink and brushed off the Cheerios, dropping the remaining vomit in the sink, squidging it down through the drain cover.

I washed my hands and arms and walked over to my bag—which was in a little cupboard next to the bed—to change my top, but the HCA came back with a second cereal bowl, half-filled. She gave me the bowl and told me that the doctors said I need to finish my breakfast.

I could not believe this. I did not want to eat, and I didn't want to vomit. I sat there in vomit-covered clothes, forcing another mouthful of cereal into my mouth. I had tears rolling down my face because I was terrified; I was going to vomit again and suffocate. I felt dirty and humiliated, especially as this was in front of the other patients in the bay.

I looked around in the hope of a vomit bowl magically appearing, but there was none. Vomit came up to my mouth, and I swallowed it back down. I continued doing this for the rest of the breakfast. The HCA sat with me for around 30 minutes after I had finished, to make sure I was not going to vomit.

This meant that I sat in vomit-covered clothing for about an hour altogether before I was allowed to wash. Up and down the food went in my food pipe. Reflux, mouth, swallow. My mouth was burning from the acid, my food pipe was on fire, but as long as I didn't vomit, the HCA would go. As long as I kept swallowing my own vomit, I would not choke.

I focused on one spot to get myself through this; I focused so hard. I knew I could get through this, as tears continued to roll down my cheeks.

This was the first time I disassociated. To cope, I felt a big mental barrier between me and the nurse. This was the first time I remember it happening.

After 30 minutes, she got up and walked out, telling me she had actual patients to look after. I got my clean top, went into the bathroom, vomited and changed my top.

When I got out of the bathroom, a nurse asked me if I had vomited in the toilet. I denied it. I didn't know what was happening, but it felt like the right thing to do. I didn't want any more breakfast, I didn't want to have to go through that again, and I did not want to vomit.

I was then allowed to go to hospital school and then got back to bed for lunchtime. Routinely, I was not having lunch as I was fairly reliant on my feeds, and I presumed that it was okay. I had only vomited twice with my feeds that day. So, when they called our room for food. I politely declined.

The HCA from earlier told me that I did not have a choice and that I was going down with her to pick my lunch. I explained I wasn't hungry with the feed. It was more that I didn't want to experience what I experienced earlier, although I did not tell them this. She went away and brought back a doctor.

'Kayleigh, if you do not try, there are ways we will feed you without your permission.'

I looked up at this doctor whom I had never met before and was blindsided. I didn't understand why they were being so mean. Why are they threatening me? I already felt like they were force-feeding me. They were an adult, and I was a child who was alone and vulnerable.

I felt vulnerable. I just could not understand why everyone had turned on me and why people were choosing to let me suffer. I had not done anything wrong. I had reflux.

Terrified of being force-fed against my will, *just being force-fed within my will,* I just nodded and followed the HCA. There was a choice of lots of different foods on their food wagon, and I picked up chicken and tomato pasta.

The same HCA sat down opposite me, and I picked at the food. I was trying to make it look like I had eaten more than I had; moving it around my plate, eating small mouthfuls, spending time cutting things up.

Once the HCA was happy with the amount I had eaten. She walked off. About one and a half hours later, I refluxed everything into the toilet, but I did not tell anyone.

My dad came in the afternoon, we played a game of cards, and he brought sherbet lemons. Dad only liked playing card games he could win; he refused to play snap, he said I was brutal at it. I just thought because I was quicker and had a better chance of winning. I was very unhappy about the day, but I tried to pretend that everything was fine, and for a little while it was.

Dinner time was always soups and sandwiches. I was okay to have soup, as it was easy to go down and come up, but I was avoiding all breads as they got stuck in my throat. A nurse came this time to collect me to go to the food trolley. I walked down, dragging my feet, trying to prolong the walk as much as possible.

Vegetable soup or carrot and coriander; I chose vegetable. She filled the bowl to the top. They were crazy if they thought I could eat all of that, but at least it's not a sandwich. She placed the bowl onto the tray, and I turned to walk away.

'No, Kayleigh, you need to choose a sandwich too.'

I stopped.

I couldn't eat a sandwich, they get stuck in my throat and become painful, that's too much, I thought to myself.

'I don't want a sandwich, this soup will be enough,' I replied, trying to sound as persuasive as possible.

'No, Kayleigh, remember what the doctor said earlier?'

A flashback to the strange man telling me:

'There were other ways of getting me to eat without my permission.'

I had vivid images of them holding me down and stuffing my mouth full of ham sandwiches, and me choking and suffocating. A twang of panic hit my stomach like a bolt and ran through my body. I refluxed pure acid, swallowing it quickly, causing my eyes to flood with tears.

'Please, a sandwich is too much,' I begged.

The nurse shook her head. She agreed to half a sandwich but nothing less. Going from pretty much not eating and relying on feeds to nearly three meals, including food that was difficult, in a day seems bizarre. Literally like running before you could walk. It would only set you up for failure.

But who could I complain to? The doctors were talking about force-feeding, and Mum and Dad had agreed to this treatment. I was alone in this. As I walked back to my bed, tears rolled down my face. I sobbed into my soup, and I got away with only eating half. I then started on the sandwich.

The first mouthful was not too bad, but the second mouthful got stuck in my throat. I took a drink to start pushing it down, and that got stuck. I took another mouthful, and that worsened the situation.

The pain that radiated from my chest felt like it was exploding, and then my stomach started refluxing, causing the pressure to mount even more. I needed a vomit bowl; I looked around, and there was none there.

I called the nurse, 'I need to vomit.'

She responded, 'You don't, Kayleigh. You just think you do.'

This sandwich was clawing its way out of me, and vomit bowl or not, it was coming out of me, whether I liked it or not. As it exited my mouth, I pointed my head to the bed. I was not trying to aim anywhere; I just didn't want to be left sitting in my own vomit again.

As I vomited, I started choking, and I couldn't breathe. The nurse ran over and hit me hard on my back. Tears were streaming down my face from my eyes, my nose was running, I had vomit-choked so hard that bits of soup were coming from my nasal passages, and my tube also came out of my mouth.

After the last reminiscence of dinner exited from my mouth and nose, I wiped my face with the sleeve of my top, and I curled up in a ball on the chair and cried. I told them I couldn't have sandwiches. Why did they not believe me? I didn't understand. They changed my bed sheets in time for Mum to come and stay over.

That day had been my worst so far as a patient, and that night, as usual, Mum fell asleep as soon as her head hit the pillow. I tried to stay up all night because then it would be ages for the morning and for breakfast. If I fell asleep, breakfast would be sooner. I lay on the bed, looking at the decorated ceilings, crying to myself, until I dropped off to sleep.

* * * *

The next morning, they did not wake me up for breakfast, but I woke up naturally as the doctors came around. They spoke about how well I did in the afternoon with no vomiting. Mum's face beamed when she heard, like music to her ears.

How could I tell her I vomited? How could I ruin her day like that? They did say that I had found the sandwiches particularly difficult, so for the time being, it was okay to not have them—silver lining, right?

Lunchtime soon came around, and I was marched down to the food trolley to eat. I had pasta again with mince. I took mice steps on the way back to prolong the time before I tried to eat. Mouth full after mouth full, a different HCA sat staring at me, making sure I was eating it.

'See, it wasn't that hard,' she said in a condescending but trying to seem nice way.

It was like everyone had been handed out a book on how to be a bitch to Kayleigh. Why were people being like this? The thing was that she could not feel the acid going up and down my oesophagus. She sat with me for 15 minutes quietly. I focused on my one spot again, but I could not take it anymore; I needed to vomit.

I ran to the sink and heaved all up. There were no vomit bowls; I had no choice. I didn't want to vomit over myself, and the nurses had made such a fuss yesterday when they changed the bed sheets. The sink was the only other option.

It turned out the staff had deliberately removed the vomit bowls from the bay, as they did not want me to be reminded about vomiting.

'Why did you do that, Kayleigh? Do you not want to get better?' she almost shouted at me.

I felt so guilty and embarrassed. Of course, I wanted to get better, but I had no control over it. Why did they think I did?

Over the following days, this continued; it was hell. I was berated for vomiting. I was being forced to eat and vomit. I had no control. I did not understand why the hospital wanted me to suffer. Each day was torturous; I was being shouted at, talked down to, and I was vomiting over myself, my bed, the table, and then victimised when I did vomit.

I had to tell people when I went to the toilet and what I did in the toilet. They would ask me if I had vomited. It was nearly always yes, but I could not admit to it, or they would give me the food again. To limit my suffering, I would say no.

They would then double-check because they didn't believe me and, in all fairness, this was the only thing they were right about. I was not going to admit it, though. The mental anguish was impenetrable. The suffering was overwhelming, and I felt completely on edge; like everyone was out to get me.

I had not been sleeping, which worsened my mental health. I was frozen in fear, making choices became difficult, but the nurses took this as me being difficult and not mentally struggling due to their actions. It caused them to be mean and unkind. Worsening my situation.

One evening, I went to the toilet and vomited. The staff found out, and the next morning, I was accused of hiding my vomiting. This made the situation worse; my every step was accounted for. If I breathed, they documented it; if I dropped an eyelash, it was documented.

I could not go to the toilet without an explanation. The nurses and other health care staff were cold to me. The play assistant told me off for talking about vomiting. Every person had changed to me.

I would be left to vomit into my hands, bins and sinks. The only grace was that after a week, they allowed me to vomit into a vomit bowl, but only if I asked. They stopped my feeds during the day with the hope of making me hungry and want to eat as well.

Each night I lay on my bed, crying to myself, choosing not to sleep so that morning was far away. I was exhausted, and I found myself trying to understand why people were being so mean; why people wanted me to suffer.

I didn't understand why they were threatening me with force-feeding. Why were people making me sit in vomit? Why was I being punished in such a humiliating way? I didn't want to be ill. I never chose this life.

It felt all-encompassing, there was no rest bite, there was no break, it felt never-ending. All the adults in my life had turned against me, and I had no one to turn to. I felt helpless. It felt like there was no adult fighting my battle. I felt alone and isolated. Within six months, my life had turned on its head.

I was a healthy 10-year-old, and now I was in the hospital being force-fed. I felt hopeless. I could not see a happy ending, no surgery. I could feel Mum and Dad's sadness, and it was my fault. It felt like all the happiness in the world had gone, and I was alone.

I prayed each night that I would not wake up in the morning, because my prayers about getting better had not been heard. In the same breath, I wished that Dr Zhang could save me.

If I look back now, it broke my heart to think that I was 11 years old and begging God to die. I don't even think I knew what suicide was; I just knew what death was, and I knew that people didn't suffer in death, they went to heaven. That's what I wanted, peace.

My mental health over this time was incredibly bad. I remember crying myself to sleep. I remember praying, begging for this to be better. I remember praying to not be here in complete desperation. I remember wanting not to be here with every cell in my body. I felt like I could not live like this. There was no hope. It was so hopeless and so isolating.

I only found out two weeks ago (whilst writing this) that I had never been diagnosed with a mental illness. Only that the psychotherapist had said that there was a behavioural element to my vomiting, which was why they started undertaking this treatment.

This angers me as the treatment I received was above and beyond what I was diagnosed with. I should never have been treated the way I was. This period in my life impacted my relationship with my parents. As an adult, I completely understand why they agreed to this treatment, because if they had said no, they could have lost me to the system.

However, from my perspective, my parents agreed me being abused by the staff. I don't use the word abuse lightly, but their (the healthcare workers') actions towards me caused me significant emotional and psychological pain. I felt like my parents had given up on me.

That they could not love me if they wanted me to suffer like this. I felt completely isolated and alone. A fracture appeared in my relationship with my parents.

* * * *

Three weeks, this went on. I was completely desperate, completely broken. I was outright suicidal. I could not breathe without having it documented. I felt vulnerable and I felt hopeless.

On a Thursday afternoon, one of the ward doctors came running in with a piece of paper in her hand.

'Kayleigh, I have some news!'

I could see from her that she was happy.

'Greengate called us this morning and I have already told your mum. Your specialist said that your stomach lining had grown a bug called H. Pylori.'

I shook my head; she needed to explain more.

'It's a bug that can grow in your stomach, and it's treatable. It could be the cause of all your troubles.'

I almost instantly felt like the weight that was crushing my chest lifted off. It felt like the storm that had been sitting over my head was now sunny. Everything looked brighter and happier. I felt like God had answered my prayers. It felt like a miracle.

Almost instantly, the staff were being nice again. I no longer needed to be watched when eating; I could vomit freely. There was an abundance of vomit bowls. I just needed antibiotics, which were started the following day.

They even allowed me to draw and paint on one of the ceiling boards in the children's ward. I painted a 3D aquarium and was so proud of my artwork.

Years later, I visited the ward and was so sad to see them all removed. I couldn't begin to tell you how happy I was to have it up there even briefly. Because it was the first thing I woke up to in the morning and the last thing I fell asleep to at night. I would look at them through all my procedures, too. It was a comfort.

The relief I felt from this new diagnosis was like a heated blanket in a blizzard, just wonderful. I slept for 18 hours as I finally felt like I was safe after three weeks of hell. When I next saw Mum, she gave me such a big hug, which was full of complete relief. A relief that she also felt.

Years later, I told Mum what had happened, and she admitted she was unaware of the severity of the treatment that I was experiencing, as she was away when it was eating time. She was just under the impression they were going to offer me food.

No one ever apologised for the treatment.

I would need to take the medication for two weeks. They prepared it for me, and I was allowed to be discharged home after two days. I stopped vomiting and was cured.

The end.

I f**king wish—

* * * *

All my hospital letters say that my vomiting improved once I commenced on clarithromycin and metronidazole—the antibiotics.

I wish that I could say that it did. I don't remember deliberately hiding my vomiting; it had become a bit of a habit with the treatment I had been receiving recently. I had started to become anxious every time I vomited because I was terrified of being told off.

So, hiding vomiting from people who don't want to see you vomiting was fairly easy. But as the vomiting continued. I was soon readmitted with weight loss and dehydration.

When Mum told me I needed to go to the hospital, I had a tantrum that 2-year-olds would be proud of; begging and pleading to Mum and Dad not to go to the hospital, but they drove me there.

This reinforced in my mind that Mum and Dad were against me. They were forcing me to go to a place I no longer felt safe in, the hospital, where I was experiencing mentally traumatic treatment.

Every time I was readmitted, it seemed to reinforce the mental health diagnosis in the doctors' and nurses' minds, but they had stopped walking me to the dinner trolley and watching me. Instead, they would just offer food and write *declined* across my notes.

I was terrified to eat in the hospital because if I were sick, I would stay longer, or worse, I was worried that they would start with the pressure feeding again. I was in a state of constant anxiety, and I was on edge. I just did not understand why they were doing this to me, because I just had reflux and was now treated for H. Pylori.

However, because I chose not to eat on the ward, this further pushed the doctors to believe it was mental health, and they started treating me for a *food phobia.*

Looking back now, I did need mental health support. Not for a food phobia or behavioural problem, but for support going through this awful time. As a disabled adult (spoiler alert), this time continues to impact my treatment and my relationships with doctors and medical staff. This continued to haunt me to this day.

I remember being so angry at everyone. The hospital, my parents, the whole situation. I had no control over my life; all the happiness had been sucked away, and I was in this vacuum of awfulness. There was no way out.

* * * *

Kate was a middle-aged lady. She was calm, firm and nice. She had brown hair and brown eyes, and she always wore smart but comfortable-looking clothes. I didn't trust her. I knew what her lot were about; they would twist my words against me, like they did at Greengate.

She was a community psychiatric nurse. She was going to treat me with cognitive behavioural therapy (CBT) for a food phobia.

Before meeting Kate, Mum spoke to me about the importance of putting on a united front.

She would say to me, 'You have a physical condition, Kayleigh. They just need to know it.'

She never told me what to say, but she advised me to be careful with how I presented myself and what I talked about. But I knew this, I had learnt my lesson.

Kate was the enemy, and she held all the power. Each week, I visited her and we spoke about my relationship with food. Which automatically improved once I was at home, and once I was not being forced into eating. She asked me about my mood, and I told her I was *okay*.

I never really understood what CBT was for or why they were doing it, but I went along with it. If I didn't, the doctors would tell me I was being difficult, and it would cement that my condition was a mental health one, even further. It felt like I had to ride the waves just to prove my physical condition.

My family were drained with all the to-ing and fro-ing from hospital and appointments. We were worn out. My mum and dad had aged in the last four months. We were a shell of what we had been. Sarah was just pushing through. *I was always astounded by how well she did.*

In the back of my mind, I did start questioning myself. Maybe I was crazy. Maybe this was what crazy feels like. I mean, we had mental illness in the family, my uncle and dad. Maybe this was my crazy.

I know that crazy is not the most politically correct term, but I did not know that then.

The logical side of my brain would argue that I had never made myself sick. That I never gained anything from all the attention, and that if anything, I was jealous of Sarah's normalcy.

I knew this, but I felt like no one else did.

The doctors didn't.

The nurses didn't.

I was not sure about my parents because they would say they believed me, yet took me to a mental health unit for CBT therapy and allowed the doctors to treat me like they did. Our relationship continued to fracture.

The more I spoke to Kate, the more I started to trust her, although I didn't want to trust her. I wanted to tell her everything. I wanted to tell her that I never made myself sick; that I was terrified of having to vomit in the hospital because of how I had been treated. The fact that death seems like a retreat.

I thought she had an insight into how I was feeling, she gave me leaflets about the Samaritans and teen emergency support. This made me feel like I was failing at even hiding my feelings. If Mum knew, she would be angry. Kate kept telling me it was okay to feel low, but I continued to trust no one.

On one of my admissions, the doctors in North Surrey Hospital started talking about sending me to a specialist hospital—another one for a more specialist inpatient type service, if the *reintroduction of food treatment* that Kate was giving me didn't work.

They restarted walking me to the food trolley, watching me eat and documenting everything. It was as though they were trying to catch me out. I was in constant fear that the force-feeding was going to start. I was in constant fear that something worse was going to happen.

They were doing daily weights, measuring everything that went in me and everything that came out of me. Then they tried to stop me from vomiting. Hiding the bowls, telling me off again, distracting me when I was being sick, but not actually stopping me from vomiting. The desperation and isolation this treatment caused me to feel were indescribable.

Which is difficult when you are writing a book.

I was completely alone, and the one person who should have been there to support me as a child living with a long-term condition (Kate), I could not open up to her. Just in case she found out that I was mentally ill (with depression and anxiety, NOT an eating disorder) and made everything worse.

So, I just took everything that was dished out to me, not buffered or protected by any adult. Completely alone in the world.

At this point, Mum became a possessed lady: trying to feed me, cooking all my favourite foods, buying chocolates, and crisps. Announcing what was in the fridge and leaving treats on the side. But this put even more pressure on me and further cemented that she was on their side.

Her face, the day she was told I didn't vomit (when I did), just kept popping into my head. I wanted her to smile like that at me again, but more so, I just wanted to be left alone.

At the tender age of 30, I now understand how serious the threat to my parents was. Back then, I didn't realise that they could have lost me if they didn't agree to the treatment, and I would have been sent away. However, because of this period of time, my relationship with my parents was changed forever; we lost our spark, our happiness.

The feeling of complete isolation, and that even my parents had turned on me. I truly believed that it was no longer us against the world. It was Kayleigh against the world, and I felt it.

* * * *

I was discharged again after being rehydrated. The only benefit of the mental health team was that they had recommended that I start getting back to a normal routine, with the hope that this would change my behaviour and expose me to foods in other ways.

The school also agreed that I could go with my tube. Mum had arranged that I would go for a visit one Thursday afternoon. That morning, I had a bath and put my uniform on, which was even looser than I remembered.

Mum and I drove in, and in true Mum fashion, we were late. I signed in at reception and headed to my form. I got there as they had just started leaving for their afternoon lessons.

'KAYLEIGHHHH!'

I was mobbed by 30 school girls running to hug me. It was such a welcome. I felt joy for the first time in a long time. I was fussed over and loved. My form tutor welcomed me back and advised my form that they would be late. I went to my first proper lessons in eight months, double science, where we spent the afternoon learning about planets.

I had a brief feeling of normalcy, and I loved it. Mum came and picked me up at the end of the day, and we went home. I had felt on cloud nine. I could not wait to return again. Mum and my head of year made a plan to return to school, undertaking part-time hours, and for a few weeks, until my next admission. I felt semi-normal.

I would need to be connected to my feed at school; luckily, it all fit in a little bag that I would carry around on my back.

People at school did not seem to care much for the tube. I had one person stop me to ask me if I had Crohn's—it was a bowel disease that I had heard about from another patient at Greengate.

One time, a teacher came up behind me and told me that the bag I was using (the one for my feed) was not the school bag. As I turned around, she saw the tube across my face and the giving set connected to the bag; her face dropped. My friends were outraged, but I thought it was funny. The teacher was mortified.

Once a person asked me if I had spaghetti up my nose. I thought they were trying to be funny, but I did not get it.

I was also asked if my tube went into my nose and the other end of the tube into my bowel. Confused, I asked her to repeat what she had asked. She pointed out that the tubing on one side went into my nose.

She then followed the tube down where it had connected to the giving set and pointed out that it went into my skirt. I explained that the giving set went to my bag, not my bowel, and she seemed happy with this response.

I remember only one time that the machine beeped during a lesson, and I had to sort it out. It was during an English class, and with the teacher's permission, I left the room to sort it out.

I did, on one occasion, make the machine beep, to leave class early—I was a teenager after all.

Looking back, I still couldn't begin to describe the joy I felt being back at school. My world had been so hard, but going to school reminded me that I was not alone; I had a roomful of girls who missed me. I was happy at school.

The occasions I went to school during this time were my happiest. Little glimpses of normality. I bumped into my high school head teacher on a train once as an adult, and she asked me if the school was too hard on me. I told her no, but what I wanted to tell her was that school was a rest bite for my crazy world.

* * * *

In April 2005, I turned 12. We acknowledged the day with gifts, and we went bowling, but it was difficult to navigate a birthday when you're not eating much/vomiting lots. I just wanted my family around me, and I was happy with that.

It was difficult for my family too. My family were fairly sociable, and my parent had always thrown a little party, but this was when the main person was unable to eat; eating in general feels awkward. They made me feel special, though, and that's all I could ask for.

Out of the blue, towards the end of my hospital stay, I received a letter that Mum brought in from home. I looked at the envelope and saw nicely squiggled writing on the front. Eager to find out who this letter was from, I ripped the envelope open and read it.

The letter was from my music teacher from primary school. She was wishing me the best and that she hoped I was feeling better. That letter made me feel so special as she had gone out of her way to send me that. I wrote her a letter back, but found it in a pile of rubbish at home two years later.

In May 2005, I had a further endoscopy with St Alice. This showed severe erosive oesophagitis in multiple layers of my stomach lining. It also showed inflammatory changes with the eosinophils and focal erosions. *I have no idea what this means either, other than it's bad.*

We were informed by Dr Zhang that he believed this confirmed severe reflux.

North Surrey Hospital, however, believed this just showed that I was vomiting a lot, but that it was caused by my mental health.

The endoscopy also confirmed that my H. Pylori was treated and was negative.

This felt hard because it was confirmation that this was not the cause of my ongoing symptoms.

North Surrey Hospital did not seem to understand that they were doing more harm than good. As far as they were concerned, my eating phobia was improving, but because I was still vomiting, it was clear I still had behavioural issues. They referred me to another dietitian who asked me to fill out a food diary.

This felt just like another way of them controlling me at home. I was not very compliant with this, but Mum filled out bits of what she had witnessed. This just caused me to hide my eating from my mum. My non-compliance further cemented the *behavioural issues* diagnosis.

I was still regularly being admitted to North Surrey Hospital, but their new plan was that the second I was hydrated, I needed to go home, as they did not want to prolong a break from routine and undo all the good work.

I liked this plan better as it meant I did not stay in the hospital for long periods of time, and where possible, I could go to school. I continued to see Kate and continued to see the dietitian. Most importantly, I looked forward to seeing Dr Zhang, as we believed he had all the answers.

Mum and Dad continued to go to church; I thought it was a comfort to them. Every Sunday, there was a bit of normalcy, and they could talk to their friends about how the week had gone. Like friendship therapy. I did not go to church if I could help it. I don't think I was having a crisis of faith. I thought it was more that I was a teenager and the church was not cool.

Plus, I didn't like the fact that people asked after me, because I would then feel the need to update them, and I was a private person; I didn't want everyone and anyone to know.

I do see the irony of saying I am a private person, but then writing a book about it.

One particular Sunday, I had been dragged to church by Mum and Dad, as I had not wanted to go.

Mum had asked if I would stay to go to the club afterwards because it would be nice for people to see me, considering they were praying for me. I reluctantly agreed but said I would only show my face, then walk home. We agreed on this compromise.

Mum and Dad were sitting at the table, and I joined them for a bit before deciding that I was done and wanted to go home. I told Mum and headed out. Just as I was about to leave, I bumped into a girl from my primary school. We exchanged pleasantries, and I asked her how she was.

She responded that she was fine. She then asked me if I was nervous about an upcoming hospital test. I said I didn't know what she was talking about. She repeated herself again, and I said that as far as I knew, I was not having that investigation again before saying our goodbyes and leaving.

Two days later, I had that investigation. Mum had told her friends about what I was doing, and they had gone on to tell their children. The issue was that she had not told me.

Yes, Mum should have told me first, and she would not have expected me to hear it from an old school acquaintance. It made me feel really exposed, like everyone knew about me; like I had no privacy. I started hating going to church because everyone knew more about me than I did.

Although I had not spoken to Mum about my mental health, I was worried that she knew and had told everyone about it. I felt like a pig on display for everyone to see. The hospital had me on display; my parents had me on display; the church had me on display. I had no privacy.

On school days, I would not eat before or at school, because of the risk of vomiting. I was worried someone would see me vomit at school and people would think I was bulimic—I had picked this word up from the hospital. I didn't quite know what it meant, other than you made yourself sick to be skinny.

I couldn't understand why people would want to make themselves sick. So, I definitely didn't want people to think that I had it.

At this time, I was still allowed to undertake sports related to my field. In PE, one time I did a forward roll and my feed disconnected from my tube, spraying milk all over the mat. From then on, I disconnected from PE, not that I had told Mum or the doctors. I was worried they would tell me off as they would see it as an excuse not to be on feed.

In PE one hot afternoon, as part of our warm-up one day, we were asked to do laps of the field. Now I have never been a runner, in fact, far from it. I remember after the third lap, I was feeling really, really unwell.

I couldn't hear or see anything and felt like I was going to collapse. I told the teacher that I had not eaten and I had to sit out the rest of the lesson. From then on—no PE for me.

I started being able to travel home from school on the bus. I felt so adult with this new responsibility. My cousins would, on occasion, travel home with me too, so I felt safe and loved. One time, I was ill and went home early. My cousins were waiting for me. After this, they stopped, but I would still see them now and then.

With my tube, I was a bit of a target on the two buses I had to take home. Teens sometimes would point at it or loudly talk about it. Younger children and sometimes adults would stare at it. *I was never offered the disabled seat, though.*

For me, it was water off a duck's back. I was not bothered because my travelling home was a great achievement considering what I had been through.

One journey home, on a particularly over packed bus, where we were squeezed in like sardines. A man stood very close behind me and whispered in my ear, 'Just how I like my ladies, crippled and young,' he was so close that I smelt the alcohol on his breath.

I was shocked to the core, as he said that, he slid his arm down my waist to the top of my thigh. I was petrified to the spot, all the hairs on my arms and neck stood on end, and vomit came to my mouth.

I do think this was the most perfect time to have vomited on a stranger like a protective weapon or an animal with a sting in their tail. Also, it's disabled, not crippled...keep up with the times!

I looked around the bus to see if anyone saw. I caught a lady's eye, and she quickly looked away. I knew in that moment that I was not going to talk about it again. I got home and had a bath, as I could smell that man on me.

I have since had many experiences with men and boys, and the in-between with regards to my conditions, maybe another book's worth! Following this incident, I stopped taking this bus and chose to walk to another stop instead. I never wanted to see that man again; he made me feel so uncomfortable.

Mum had also let me go back to do my Irish dancing with Sarah on the Saturday. It would tire me out, but I enjoyed being normal. I also liked the fact that the teachers treated me the same as everyone else. One weekend, we had an Irish dancing feis (pronounced Fesh). It was a competition, and both Sarah and I competed.

Sarah got a trophy and we were so proud of her. At the end of the awards ceremony, the teacher explained that one of our dancers had been going through a lot but still turned up to dance when she could, with a big smile on her face, and she never complained at all.

I didn't realise she was talking about me until she said my name. I was so happy. Everyone in the room clapped for me as I went up to get this special trophy. Mum placed it on the mantelpiece next to Sarah's.

On one hand, it was so lovely to be acknowledged for what I was going through, but I always felt bad for Sarah as it took away her achievement too. She should have been in the spotlight; she had won a trophy for her actual skill, whereas I had just turned up.

Mum told me that it's a mark of my grit and resilience. Although I wasn't experiencing any of these feelings, it was a really kind gesture.

We soon started to attend St Alice A&E instead of North Surrey Hospital, as my gastric specialist was there.

The A&E was similar to the North Surrey Hospital one; there was a big adult A&E and then a children's A&E connected to it. The waiting room was filled with so many toys, I remember thinking that I would have loved it here when I was younger.

The beds in the A&E were split up with curtains, and one or two had their own room. The curtains were filled with yellows, reds and oranges with animals printed on them.

The first time I attended A&E, I met a nurse called Sally, who had brown hair and kind brown eyes. Her aura was pure kindness, and I started looking out for her when I attended A&E. We called her the nice nurse. It was night and day with the treatment I was experiencing from St Helier compared to North Surrey Hospital.

All the admissions I had over the years, we would look out for the nice nurse. One day, we bumped into her in the local ASDA. It felt like seeing a teacher out in the wild. It was really strange, but she remembered me and made such a fuss of me.

My first admission, I was given a cannula and placed in a wheelchair, whilst Sally pushed me up to the ward. The children's ward was connected to the main hospital by a long basement corridor. The corridor was spooky, especially at night, as noises reverberated down the hall, sounding ghost-like.

We took the lift to the second floor, which was St Alice's ward. It was one long hall split into the ward and then the day unit. The ward had three bays: elephant, where the older children went; monkeys, where the little children went; and the lion's room, where the babies went. There were a number of side rooms, too.

Usually, for the cystic fibrosis (CF) cases as they had a specialist doctor there. The décor was dated, and the paint on the wall was chipping, but it was a much happier place. The nurses were friendly, and mostly, no one was forcing me to eat or to vomit.

St Alice was an interesting place; they had the usual broken bones, appendices, but with the CF kids, it was a little more homely, a bit more like a community feel. The patients obviously trusted the nurses and doctors, so it felt like the environment was just better.

* * * *

The first time I was admitted onto the ward, I was being wheeled to Elephant Bay, and we looked up to see our postman of many years standing in the hall. He recognised us straight away and said hello.

His name was Dave, and he was one of the friendliest men I had ever met, always with a smile and a hello, no matter the weather. We told him about what was happening with me, and he stood there and listened. We went on to ask him why he was there.

He explained that his partner, Sue, had a child called Brodie who was a patient there. We were then greeted by Sue, who had blonde hair which went down to her shoulders and one of the biggest smiles I had ever seen; it literally lit up the room.

We were introduced to Brodie, who was in the bed opposite mine. She looked around 14 and had bright red hair and bluest eyes. She had a condition called early onset Huntington's disease and was unable to walk, talk or eat anymore. Next to her was her adaptive wheelchair, which was bright pink and fluffy.

Sue gave us the biggest welcome. She showed Mum where everything was, and we settled into the ward.

Whilst we were both patients, Dave would hand-deliver our post to Mum when he came to visit Brodie. Both Sue and Dave never had a bad word or felt sorry for their situation. Over the years, I watched the couple face some of the worst situations a parent could possibly deal with, and they faced them with poise, dignity and not a complaint.

Brodie died a few years later, surrounded by people she loved and who loved her. The passion, care and love that Sue and the rest of the family provided were inspirational. Nothing was too hard for Sue; she was like Wonder Woman, surrounded by people who supported her.

By the time I met Brodie, she was unable to really communicate, and due to this, I was unable to connect with her. I used to wonder what she was like when she was not disabled and what her personality was like.

I later learnt that she loved playing with her cousins, just like me. I watched from afar as the cruel disease ate away at her brain, and she was in and out of the hospital for the rest of her life.

Dave disappeared from our postal route suddenly after Brodie died. We didn't know what happened and thought he had moved on to greener pastures. Around 15 years later, I was attending my cousin's baby shower, and who should I bump into but Sue and Dave?

My cousin was about to marry their nephew. We spent the afternoon catching up and chatting about Brodie (and obviously the new baby to be, too). It was so lovely.

* * * *

A week later, I was discharged and Mum and Dad decided to treat Sarah and me, so they booked a little holiday for three days in Jersey—the Channel Islands. It gave us something to look forward to.

Early on Friday morning, we packed all our things into the car, one small bag for Sarah, one small bag for Mum and a rucksack for Dad.

For me, however, I had a clothes bag, an auxiliaries bag, a feed box and the family microwave (all I was eating were these microwave noodles as they were easy to go down and come up. The hotel did not have a microwave in the rooms so this seemed like the logical thing to do—kind of.)

We drove for two and a bit hours to Portsmouth to get the boat over. Both Sarah and I were so excited; it was a chance to be normal for a bit. Mum and Dad needed the break too. We drove onto the ferry and found a nice table to base ourselves whilst we took turns looking at the shops.

The journey between Portsmouth and Guernsey went without an issue. Sarah, Dad and I started playing cards, and it felt like we were normal again—with Dad cheating and me getting annoyed at the injustice—as I played the part of faux annoyance whilst Sarah giggled at the faux drama.

The captain announced, 'The waters are rough between Guernsey and Jersey, and if you are feeling sick, please use the vomit bags provided and not use the toilets.'

Rough would not even cover it. The boat felt like God himself had picked up the boat and started shaking it. Everyone was sick, including the staff. There were filled paper bags of vomit everywhere. Everyone had turned green and sweaty.

The smell of vomit was in the air. Ignoring the captain's words, the toilets were unusable due to vomit lasagne clogging up the loos. It was a mess! Mum, Dad and Sarah had placed their heads on the table where we were sitting in desperation of trying to counteract the swaying of the boat.

I, on the other was not affected at all. I walked around the boat, went up and got fresh air. In fact, my cheerful behaviour seemed to make Mum and Dad more annoyed.

There was a problem, though, as the vomit bags that everyone used were made out of paper. They slowly disintegrated, and as we came into dock, they started exploding like little bombs made out of vomit. The smell was stomach-churning. When the captain said we could return to our cars, we ran; anything to get off that boat!

When we arrived at our chain hotel, we tried to sneak the microwave into the room. However, we had to pass the receptionist, who saw the microwave and stopped us. Mum explained the situation, hoping they were going to be flexible, but they said no.

Something to do with it not being PAT tested, and due to that was a fire hazard. We asked whether it could then get tested, but that was a no, too. Mum started to worry as she said that I would not be able to eat. As a compromise, the chef said he would heat my special food up, and Mum relaxed.

For the next three days, we felt like a family again; we laughed and joked, we bickered and made up. We went on little adventures. It was healing time. It was wonderful.

On the final day, I woke up in the morning to find out my feed had disconnected from my tube. The bed was soaked with this milky substance. It had gone through the sheets onto the mattress, and there was no mattress protector on it.

Mum and Dad did their best to clean the mattress, but the damage was already done. I know it wasn't my fault, but I felt very guilty, especially as the hotel had gone out of its way to help us. We apologised at the front desk, and they tried to make us feel better too.

The boat journey back was like night and day compared to the journey there; the boat hardly rocked, and it felt like we were sliding on smooth ice. As we drove back home, our happy little holiday bubble burst, and the reality of our situation weighed heavily on our shoulders once more.

* * * *

As a family, we no longer felt as though I was receiving safe treatment at North Surrey Hospital. We would now go to St Alice because Dr Zhang continued to try and find out what was wrong.

If my tube came out, I would have to go to North Surrey Hospital, though, as they had the capability to replace it; if I went to St Alice's, I would have had to go through A&E, which could take hours. One particular evening, I was sitting in the procedures room on the ward in North Surrey Hospital.

The nurses started telling me off for pulling the tube out. Mum and I explained that we were told to remove the tube after I vomited it, but she was having none of it. I could not win.

Mum and Dad were desperate to get my treatment to medical only. After a lot of searching, Mum found a specialist professor in gastroenterology at Great Ormond Street Hospital (GOSH) and we paid to see him privately—as a Hail Mary.

On the day of the appointment, Mum and Dad took me up on the bus to Great Ormond Street Hospital. We went into this office building, which did not look like a hospital. We were seen by a receptionist and then by the professor. My memory was that he was an older gentleman. Very Dumbledore—Michael Gambon Era, although looking back, he was more Uncle Vernon's age.

The professor went through my childhood history, tests, hospital letters and concluded that all my symptoms were secondary to my reflux. He explained to us that the coughing caused by the bronchitis likely weakened my muscles, causing a worsening of my symptoms.

He wrote a letter, and a week later it was delivered on the doorstep.

The letter read:

Diagnoses:

1. Gastro-oesophageal reflux disease
2. Sliding hiatus hernia
3. Grade 4 oesophagitis

Recommendation:

1. Nissen fundoplication

The relief that we instantly felt as a family was immeasurable. It felt like a f@#k you to North Surrey Hospital.

Within a week, Dr Zhang had referred me back to Greengate Hospital, and we were informed that it would take a couple of months for me to have surgery.

Dr Zhang even went on to advise me not to eat due to the severity of my refluxing, as it would reduce if I was not eating, but to keep with the feeds. This was literally the opposite of North Surrey Hospital and was very ironic.

When I was at home, I was feeding overnight and schooling during the day. However, I was having regular short-term admissions for dehydration.

* * * *

Since staying away from North Surrey Hospital, I felt better, I felt safer.

Mum, Dad and Dr Zhang continued to email Greengate, waiting for the surgery. Unfortunately, because I was in and out of the hospital and with the deterioration of my oesophagus, Dr Zhang decided that it would be more beneficial to keep me in the hospital until surgery.

This was with the hope that it would put more pressure on Greengate to do the surgery.

So, at the beginning of June 2005, I was admitted to the ward. I was placed in the elephant room, in the corner bay, by the window. The windows were very old and did not keep the wind out. The curtains would move every time there was a gust of wind. The bay had four beds, and behind each bed were dated pictures of animals on the wall.

At St Alice, there was no school room, only a teacher and this teacher was a primary school teacher. Every day, he would visit me to say hello, because we had spoken, he could tell me that I had attended school, and there would be no more interaction.

In reality, there were no classes. My school tried to send work in, but it was difficult to get to and from school, which meant that it was few and far between.

My family and I made a routine, Mum had returned to work after being away from work for nine months. She would no longer stay at night. Go to work, after work, she would visit me, in the afternoon, then go home, shower, change, eat and then go bed. Dad would visit me after work, in the evenings, before going home, eating, then going to bed. Sarah would visit on weekends.

Other than that, I was alone. I seldom got any other visitors. My cousins would come occasionally, but that would be few and far between; they were busy and had lives.

I was never angry that I did not have many visitors. I knew that I was well loved, but that coming to see me was out of everyone's way. My aunty, who was close by, was doing a lot of Sarah sitting when Dad and mum had to go into work. My other Aunts lived quite far away, but Mum and Dad kept them updated.

The first night when Mum was not sleeping next to me was scary. With Mum going back to work, she needed to sleep better and get ready for work in the morning, to ensure her patients get the best from her. I understood this, although it did not make it easier.

I would ensure my curtains were closed, and I always slept with one eye open; if anyone came within my curtained area, I would wake up. I didn't know the other patients or their parents well enough to sleep deeply, and I was in too much discomfort to sleep when the feed was on. So, it felt like I never slept.

The day-to-day routine at St Alice was similar to North Surrey Hospital. we would get up in the morning and have doctor's rounds. Then the teacher would say hello. The play specialist would then come and say hi in the afternoons.

Mum would then come, go and then Dad Mum. Breakfast, lunch and dinner would come to each bay, unlike North Surrey Hospital, where you would have to go to them.

The afternoons were quiet, if you didn't have to have investigations. I would stay busy by reading or playing Sims on a laptop. Unlike Greengate, there was no TV per bed; instead, there was an old-style box one for the whole bay, which was seldom used.

The only time I ever remember it being on was for Live Eight in 2005. One of the nurses had a crush on Robbie Williams, and she told us to pull the emergency crash alarm when he was on, and we did. She ran from one side of the ward to the other side to watch him in our bay. We laughed at the two nurses getting us up and dancing to Let Me Entertain You.

I would still be having my regular feeds and was reliant on them. If I started getting dehydrated, I would be placed on an intravenous drip (IV) via a cannula. The issue with this was that my veins were not very welcoming to the little plastic tube anymore, and the cannula would tissue often, causing pain and swelling.

It would then need to be re-sited. On average, at this time I was receiving a new cannula every three days and over time, it started to become hard to find my veins. So, there would be one or two attempts with the needle.

The days merged into one. The sun radiated onto my bed through the window during the day, and then the moon would follow suit.

* * * *

The Thursday morning started like all the others. I was disconnected from my overnight feed. The doctors came around, making sure everything was okay, and then the teacher came around to say hi.

The ward was a buzz, as it was every morning, but suddenly there was a blanket of seriousness and concern on the ward. There were whispers and people were checking their phones. The radio in the nurse's office was turned on and up. People were tearful, and emotion hung in the air.

One of the nurses came to me, as I sat on my bed, and told me that I may need to be discharged, as there had been an incident in London. The incident had been the 7/7 bombings.

Over the next few hours, patients were discharged until there were only three of us in all the bays: me, a boy who had been in a moped crash and a girl who had fractured her hip. Even some of the children in the side rooms were discharged.

The hospital staff tried to hide the brutality as it played out around the world. They turned the TVs off and muted the radios. The doctors and nurses would play down the situation, and the play therapist brought us arts and crafts to do, to distract us. However, like everyone else, we wanted to know what was happening.

I tried to call Mum, as Dad sometimes went to London, she was working in a prison at this time and did not have her phone. Eventually, she called back, telling me Dad was fine.

However, it was still scary as he would have to come home from London, and we didn't know if there were any more attacks planned. Mum tried to calm my fears, but I could tell by her voice she had the same concerns.

My only understanding of a terrorist attack was 9/11, and I knew thousands had been killed, and my heart hurt with what was happening. I tried to get as much information as I could, but the adults shielded us from the worst of it.

It didn't hide the fact that they were emptying the children's ward; did they expect children to be injured? How many would need to be injured for them to come to a hospital in the suburbs of London? That day, everyone held their breath, like the world had been paused, the anticipatory silence before a storm. Luckily, the storm never came.

As the day went on, the ward was eerily quiet. It was only until the late afternoon, I was told I was not being discharged, and over the next day, they started admitting patients again, and life on the ward soon sprang back to normal.

When I next saw Mum, she told me that the bus that exploded was the same bus that Mum, Dad and I had taken to GOSH three weeks earlier. My heart dropped out of my feet.

* * * *

Towards the end of August, my letter came:

'We are pleased to invite Miss Kayleigh for surgery on 28 September 2005, for a keyhole Nissen fundoplication operation. Please come on the 27th, so we can undertake pre-surgery tests, and you will be nil by mouth from midnight.'

Mum skipped onto the ward with this letter in her hand; she was so happy, and so was I. My cure. We could put this all behind us, and life would be good. Life would go back to normal.

I stayed in the hospital for a few more weeks, but Dr Zhang let me go home a few days before, so I could sleep in my own bed. I was on cloud nine. I was going to be cured!

On 27 September, Mum and I travelled by public transport to Greengate Hospital. I was admitted into a side room with a big glass window overlooking the entrance of the hospital, and I felt a bit like a goldfish.

I have to be honest; I remember very little about that night other than nerves and anxiety. I had pre-surgery bloods and tests. I remember looking out the window, once Mum had gone to the parent hotel, and bawling my eyes out with anxiety and nerves, but also happiness. I remember thinking I had to be strong.

My consultant came in the morning. He spent time explaining what was going to happen today and getting Mum to sign the consent for the surgery. He left to get changed, and a few moments later, the porters came to take me to the theatre.

I clenched my fists with nerves, holding my mum's hand tight as they pushed me through the *only staff beyond this point* double doors on the ward. I was taken to a little room where they connected me to the heart monitor, and my little heart was racing.

I had told them how much the anaesthetic hurt during my many endoscopies, so they put me to sleep with gas. They asked me to count down from 10 to one, whilst they held a face mask over my nose and mouth.

'10…9…8…7…6…5…5…4—'

I woke up in recovery. I had a mask on my face, I had multiple cannulas in my arm and a catheter. Plus, a blood pressure cuff, heart probes on my chest and the saturation probe on my finger. I tried to move, but my stomach hurt.

The nurse saw that I had woken up and greeted me.

'Hello, Kayleigh, it's nice to meet you. If you're in pain, press this little green button and you will get some pain relief.'

I nodded and pressed the button, and fell back asleep.

The next time I woke, I was in a different room, which was a bay with two other beds and a side room. I later found out it was HDU. I looked to my left, and my paternal grandma and granddad were sitting next to me. They did not say a word but disappeared when I fell back asleep.

I love the idea that my grandparents came to visit me in ghostly forms. Although I was sure it was the drugs I was on, the fact that I saw them brought me so much comfort. I don't even remember them when they were alive, but I knew who they were as they were just like in the photos we have around the house. They brought me peace and safety.

Post-surgery, I was in a lot of pain. They tried me on multiple medications to help with pain. The morphine caused my respiratory rate to drop, which meant that the nurses had to wake me up and remind me to breathe. It also gave me a sensation of itchy bugs crawling up my legs. I was scratching my legs so much, I drew blood.

Whilst given ketamine, I hallucinated that the Thomas the Tank Engine wallpaper turned into rhinos and the rhinos were charging at me. I also hallucinated that the nurses were on roller skates and that I was attacked by a clown. Fentanyl was best for pain management for me; I did not seem to get adverse symptoms with it.

To this day, I am still terrified of clowns.

On the second day, the nurse explained that the plan was to get me out of bed and onto the reclining seat. The reason for this was to aid in healing and reduce blood clots, reduce infections and pressure sores. A physiotherapist arrived and introduced himself. He and the nurse started preparing for me to move, took the blankets off me, and put the bed side down.

They rolled me on my side and supported me in going from lying to sitting with my legs off the bed. They took one arm each and allowed me to put my feet on the floor before standing. I took two steps before they guided me in turning.

The nurse with one hand had to support me, and the other hand was trying to untangle all the tubes and wires connected to me. I felt the chair behind me before I fell into it in an exhausted heap. I was not looking forward to getting back into bed. Whilst I was in the chair, they changed all my bed sheets.

Getting back into bed was not as hard as I thought it was going to be, although it was sorer than getting into the seat. It was technically more difficult as the tubes connected to me got into a tangle around the nurse.

Mum and Dad came and visited me that day. As a present for getting through the surgery, Mum and Dad got me Green Day's American idiot album. The nurse looking after me also happened to love Green Day and played it out loud in HDU. It was totally inappropriate, and I loved every moment.

I was the oldest child in HDU. The other child was about 5, and they had their parents next to them. The parents were okay with us playing the CD, which was nice, but I don't think they knew what it was until it was played.

On day three, I was stepped down and I went back to the main ward.

Embarrassingly, whilst I was in HDU, I developed a huge rash across my bottom and lower back, which had caused the skin to peel off. After I was assessed by a dermatologist and had a skin biopsy, it turned out I was allergic to the absorbent Inco-pads they placed under patients in critical care.

The dermatologist was so impressed with my rash that he got a professional photographer to take a photo and published an article on it. So, to this day, in some extremely niche circles, I have a famous bum! *(I still have the scar from the biopsy.)*

The next morning, the surgeon came around and explained that the surgery was long, as I had numerous adhesions, but that he repaired the hiatus hernia and completed the nission fundoplication, and everything looked great. This was the news we wanted to hear: I was cured.

The weight off my shoulder was immeasurable. I could go back to school. I could stop all these long hospital admissions. I was going to be normal again. I was going to be back to annoying Sarah. I was so happy.

That day, I slowly got up and walked about with the help of mum and the nurses. Each day was stronger and brighter. I decided on the fifth day that I was going to try some food, and I had some cheesy soft pasta, as the surgeon gave me the okay. There was no reflux! I could have danced if I were able to. I was so happy, completely on cloud nine.

Two days later, they removed my NG tube. I had tears in my eyes from the relief and freedom this gave me. I was no longer tarnished as a sick person. I was normal again. I was so happy. I had the world at my feet.

I was discharged from the hospital on 4 October I returned home. I ate anything and everything I could. I had a year's worth of food to eat. Mum and Grandma were so happy to feed me again. It was like the weight was removed from everyone. Our miracle happened. God was good.

I returned to school doing part-time hours and built my time up to full-time. I was very behind everyone, and I was so worried about getting in trouble, especially as I found it difficult to ask my teachers for help.

Unfortunately, one of the effects of being exposed to abuse is that I struggled with communicating and asking for help from people who held power. Teachers, adults in general, nurses and doctors.

Other than that, I was having a lovely time, and I'd returned to undertaking PE too, which was fun. When I was ready, I had been asked by my form tutor to play netball for our form, against one of the other forms. I was so excited and really happy I had been asked, as it made me feel like I was back and a part of the form.

I was not able to play the whole game due to pain, but I didn't care. I returned to guides on a Friday night. I picked up playing the violin, and I was even invited to a cool girl's birthday party, which Mum and Dad said I couldn't go to, something about them not knowing the girl's parents.

Not that I am still bitter about it.

My mum's co-worker put me forward for the Croydon Child of Courage award, and in October, I found out that my story was going to be in the local Guardian. A journalist called me and my mum and asked about my situation. A photographer then came to the house and took a photo of me.

I felt very special. The award ceremony was not going to be until January, though. The headline was 'Dreaming of Tasting the Delights of Food'. *It can still be found on the internet; you can see my fringe in all its glory and my sexy school uniform.*

Christmas of 2005 came, and we had a big feast. It was beautiful. It was amazing. It felt like our miracle. We did

Christmas properly, watched the ITV pantomimes on the telly the week before Christmas.

Sarah and I both attended midnight mass for the first time. The Christmas incense sent Sarah off to sleep on my shoulder, but she woke up at the end of mass. We were allowed to open one present when we got home after mass.

We went to bed and woke up early morning, excited to see what presents we got. Dad and Mum fussing over both of us as we opened them, happiness in every second of every minute. Soon, the house was filled with the smell of cooking.

We went to 11 am Christmas Day Mass too, as my parents played music for both. We wished the friends and family who were attending mass a Merry Christmas and caught up with what gifts people received. Singing the carols at the top of our lungs with Mum and Sarah, dad strumming along on his guitar.

Back at home, Mum made a feast: Turkey, with all the trimmings, parsnips, leeks with cheese and Christmas pudding. I ate everything I could, except the Christmas pudding—*still not a fan.*

In the afternoon, we visited our cousins, where we exchanged presents and played games. Mostly watched my older cousins play on their computers. We went home filled with sugar and happiness. Fell asleep early as part of our food coma.

The next day, we went to visit Dad's side of the family. We drove the hour up to Hampshire, where they now resided. Their house was in the country and overlooked a field full of horses. The whole family came over, including my uncle and my other aunt and her family.

We celebrated my cousin's birthday too, and then we ate a second feast, cracked crackers and played games before retiring to the front of the fire. That night, all the cousins slept in one bedroom, and we were up all night watching ghost stories (against my aunt's wishes).

The next morning, we were woken up to a fried breakfast and planned a long walk before we drove home. The cousins, me and Sarah were running around playing games, up until the moment we drove home.

We saw the new year in at the church's New Year's Eve party. We sang Auld Lang Syne at the top of our lungs, grabbing other people's hands and furiously shaking them because at that age, it's funny. Hyped up on Pepsi, eating all the food and pudding available. Bliss.

School started soon after that, and we got back into a routine. We were all happy, and I was thriving, the happiest I felt in years. I was still 12 but about to turn 13 and was a little bit alternative in my style, I liked wearing black and listening to rock and Indie music. I spent my nights on MSN.

I was getting the bus back from school, and I felt like an adult. I felt like a different person. Mum had returned to work and looked like a weight had come off her shoulders. Sarah was loving life as well as Dad. We all looked healthier and, in general, so much happier. We got on better as a family, and life was good.

In January, there were the Croydon Champions Awards. Mum and I had gone on a shopping trip to get a nice little outfit. I had put on weight and none of my clothes fit me anymore. I did not enjoy shopping in general.

Mum had a habit of picking one outfit, going around to five other shops before going back to the original outfit.

Which was exactly what happened. It was a nice day though, as it let Mum, Sarah and bond after a long time apart. We also had KFC lunch, which I had not had in ages and was lovely.

At the Croydon Champions Award, Mum, Dad and Sarah came. I also brought a friend from primary school. The event was very glamorous, and the mayor of Croydon was there and some other important-looking people. Everyone was very cheerful and excited as the award ceremony was taking place.

I came runner-up to a girl who had lost her arms and legs to meningitis. Fair play. I received a runner-up prize of a Woolworths gift voucher. I brought myself a CD (Keizer Chiefs) and Sarah a Brats doll and Brats car.

* * * *

In February 2006, I started noticing that on occasion, I would get a small mouthful of reflux after eating. Initially, I was horrified, but I told no one. If no one knows, it's not a problem.

Over the next few weeks, it became more frequent, and I pleaded with God that it didn't come back, and I would quickly swallow it back down and tell no one. I was not going to ruin this bliss. I was not going to be the cause of unhappiness.

One evening, we were eating spaghetti Bolognese, and during the meal, I refluxed and ran to the bathroom. I came back into the living room where my family was eating, and the atmosphere had completely changed. I watched as it dawned on Mum's face, and I watched her heart break into a million pieces.

I watched as Sarah looked up at Mum and saw the sadness on her face. My dad, more stoic, said nothing, but his aura was sad. I continued to eat, but what had been a happy, chatty meal had changed to silence.

That night, as mum tucked me in, she asked me about my vomiting, and I confirmed her worst nightmare. I was refluxing again. The next morning, I looked up at Mum, and a year's worth of stress had appeared on her face. Over the next few weeks, it slowly worsened. I was not vomiting enough to need hospitalisation, but enough to be worried.

We saw my surgeon on 28 March, who recommended an endoscopy, which I underwent on 24 April. We were seen in clinic in three weeks' time, where I was informed, I had grade 4 oesophagitis, which was the worst or top level.

I was prescribed medication and told that I should not eat at all, to protect my oesophagus. I cried on the bus home; I could not keep the sadness in. I did not want to believe it. It was like my world had fallen apart again.

On the journey home, Mum brought me to Leicester Square in London and we bought cheap same-day tickets for *Blood Brothers*. I was mesmerised by the theatre show, it's the first one I had ever seen in the West End. It lifted my spirits even though it was for a little while.

We started doing this regularly. When I had a bad London appointment, we would go to the theatre. I had seen *Fame, Footloose, Les Misérables, Billy Elliot*, to name a few. It definitely created my love of musicals I have to this day.

April came and went, and I became an official teenager at 13. I got to wear a badge and made a fuss of, but it was bittersweet as although it was a happy moment, it reflected another year of sickness.

The vomiting continued. By May, I had been seen by Dr Zhang, who recommended that I would have a repeat surgery. My heart sank. I was tired and I had started to lose weight too. Within two weeks of that appointment, I had my surgery appointment booked for 29 June at 7 am.

I was admitted again into the same room, saw the surgeon and mum signed the consent form. Then the porters came and I was wheeled away to the theatre. I woke up again in HDU and spent a few days there before going back to the ward. This time I had no Inco-pads, so no bum rash, ergo no more famous bum.

I slowly started getting up, out of bed and started attending school. One evening, the play therapist gave me and another girl called Kaylie—who had leg surgery following meningitis—a camera. We went up and down the ward taking photos of the nurses and other patients (with their permission).

Natasha had Gillian Bare, and she walked with crutches. Pete was in the hospital for Crohn's. Mohammed had been punched so hard that he had fractured his jaw and had a concussion. We had such a lovely time taking photos and bonded until they took the camera off us and printed the pictures.

I have the pictures in a scrapbook at home in the attic. I have kept in contact with Kaylie, who is also a published author. It was the first time I felt like someone treated me like a teenager; I felt like an adult.

On day four post-surgery, the doctors came around and told me the importance of starting to eat. I was very eager to start, as it meant I could go home and get on with my life. A life that I was loving before this disease happened and returned. Mum had come in for lunchtime, and we were chatting away when the food trolley came around.

I picked out tuna sandwiches. I did not usually eat bread, as I found it hard to swallow, but the mayonnaise and fish juice had been absorbed by the bread, so it was soft enough to eat.

I find foods that clump together difficult to swallow, rice, dry bread, and big chunks of meat. If I take smaller bites, eat them with copious amounts of liquid or chase with a fizzy drink would allow me to swallow them, or they would stick in my throat.

We continued to chat away as I ate. Mum was telling me about work and Sarah. Dad was coming later, and she was telling me that he was going to bring a board game —vomit.

It took me by surprise; it came up as normal, but it should not have done that. Vomit? I don't understand. I looked up at Mum, who was horrified, and my heart broke into a million pieces. Mum's heart appeared to have joined mine in its complete dissolving.

Her eyes teared up, and her skin went pale and sweaty, almost like she wanted to faint or vomit. Her soul emanated the sadness that I was feeling. In that moment, it felt like I had let her down; it felt like I had let everyone down. The walls came crashing down around me, and it felt like the end of the world. This surgery was meant to be my cure. Why was I vomiting?

That night, I closed my curtains and cried hysterically; Mum had gone, and I just needed to let the emotions out. My mood was low, my anxiety was so high. I felt hopeless, like I was never going to get better. I just couldn't understand.

Looking back at this time, it felt like all my hope had gone. I felt like this was the point I knew I was never going to get better. I felt completely and utterly hopeless, and on top of that, I felt guilty for not getting better. Did I not want it hard enough? What did I do wrong? Why did God hate me so much?

Now I appreciate that there was a fair amount of Catholic guilt mixed up with these feelings, and I know now that it was not my fault, but I felt so much guilt.

Mum told me that she had been watching her child die in front of her own eyes, and when this miracle surgery failed, she struggled with this and was completely heartbroken.

The next day, I spoke to the doctors and they planned to organise another endoscopy. I couldn't tell them how I was feeling mentally because I did not want them to go down the mental health route, so I kept all my emotions in.

Mum visited me as usual, but her eyes were still swollen from crying; however, we played happy families. When lunch came around again, whilst she was there, I declined. I could not do that to her again.

Over the next few days, I waited for the endoscopy. I declined to eat food; I was terrified I would vomit again, because I did not think I could cope with this. If I didn't eat, I would not vomit.

The day of the endoscopy, I was given anaesthetic and fell into a drug-induced sleep. I woke up expecting there to be a reason why the surgery had failed, why I was still being sick. The next morning, the doctors told me that everything was fine and that *no organic cause was found.*

This was not a surgical issue. I did not feel like my heart could break anymore with each word, but it did. I don't understand, I don't get it. Why was I vomiting?

I could not cope. I cried myself to sleep each night, and each morning I did not want to wake up. I didn't want to live like this; I didn't want to live. My heart hurt so bad. I couldn't cope.

A lady with blonde straight hair came to see me one afternoon. A few days later, she sat with me and told me that the surgeons had recommended another mental health assessment, especially as I did not want to eat and they no longer believed there was anything further that could be done surgically.

In them two sentences, it felt like I was going back to stage one, and I felt overwhelmed. I was a 13-year-old, going through the hormones that a normal 13-year-old goes through, being exposed to this beyond awful situation and now this. My resilience was at zero. I was wondering whether I was, in fact, crazy, for the surgery not to have worked.

I was so low. I thought regularly about not being alive, because then I would no longer be a burden to my family and the doctors, and I would be fixed, because in heaven, you are perfect. I was so miserable. So, when the nice doctor asked me about these feelings, I told her. It came out.

My parents were informed, and they were horrified. I was not aware that my parents were going to be told about what I had said. So, when this vulnerability came out in the open and Mum and Dad heard it and then saw it on paper, they were horrified.

'This is not my daughter,' they argued. 'You must have mixed her up with another person.'

I saw how angry my parents were. I had already failed a surgery, and now I had failed my parents even more. I said nothing. Letters went to and from the hospital. I was discharged back to the care of the CPN Kate. But I no longer wanted to participate in any more therapy.

I look back now and know it was completely the situation, the illness causing my mental health to be bad and not the other way around. However, this was not what they were looking for; they were looking to diagnose me with a mental health condition that could cause the vomiting.

The thing is, even if I were bulimic, I should not have been able to vomit after the surgery. The surgery had failed, and the doctors failed to be accountable, blaming me, a vulnerable 13-year-old.

I stopped participating in things I once enjoyed. I hated everyone and everything. I was jealous of healthy people. Why me? I was angry and moody. I could not understand what was happening. I went from the TV to the Sims, then to bed.

Mum tried to get me to eat, and I would not. She brought treats and cooked food I loved, but I couldn't eat it. The memory of her face when I vomited haunted my sleep.

School was hit and miss. I was tired all the time. I was no longer interested in participating in life, let alone school. When I actually went to school, I pretended it was happy families, but home life was dire. My friends, whom I hung around with, informed me that they had been lying to me, and although there was no big break-up, I no longer wanted to be their friend.

I refused to go to therapy with Kate, even though in my last assessment with Kate, she had explicitly said that she no longer believed the cause of my vomiting was mental health. And considering what I had been through, I was very level-headed. I refused to participate in therapy with the psychologist, too.

I felt I could only eat in secret and vomit in secret, as I would see the heartbreak on my mum's face when she saw me vomit. I knew Sarah could sense that too; she was happy at school, but I felt my presence drained the happiness from her when I was at home.

I felt like I was the cause of everybody's misery. I felt like I couldn't breathe with the stress on me. I felt like I was going crazy, and I no longer wanted to cope with it. Maybe I was crazy?

I had no pleasure in life, and I was never going to be better. I felt constantly in fight or flight mode. I felt hopeless. I felt alone, and I felt abandoned by God.

Having been diagnosed with C-PTSD 15 years later. This period of time evoked some really difficult feelings that, as an adult, I continue to struggle with, especially when the C-PTSD triggered.

These feelings could be triggered by feelings of guilt, letting people down, feeling overwhelmed and hospitals. As an adult, a therapist taught me to be compassionate to myself around these feelings, which had been really difficult, as the nightmares, reliving, and flashbacks were real.

* * * *

Christmas was coming up, and I was worried about it. There was no more cheer in our house; we were separate entities under one roof. Mum, Dad and Sarah were a unit, and then there was troublesome me.

I would argue and shout at little things. I would have tantrums at the drop of a hat; I had no control, and I thought this was a big factor in it. At night, when my door was shut and the lights were off, I cried my eyes out.

Dr Zhang had not given up on me, and in December 2006, he arranged a manometry test, which measures how often you reflux over 24 hours. They placed a tube down via my nose, and 24 hours later, they removed it. The tube was thinner than an NG tube, and it wasn't too much of an awful test. I had been in and out of the children's ward for hydration.

This particular test was completed in the day unit of the ward. Once they placed the tube, I got a box on a shoulder strap that was connected to the tube. I had to press buttons on the box if I was symptomatic and if I ate or drank. The following day, the tube was removed, and we went back home to our sadness vortex.

The following Thursday, we got a call at about 8.30 pm, Mum nearly hung up as she thought it was a salesperson; it was Dr Zhang. I watched her speak to him. I knew it was Dr Zhang as her voice went from *get off my phone line* to *posh* in 0.001 second. She nodded, and the biggest smile went across her face.

She hung up the phone and relayed the information to Dad and me. She was so happy. He called to explain that over a 24-hour period, I have refluxed 342 times, including when I was asleep and that the only next step was to have another nission fundoplication and that I was no longer allowed to eat again, to limit my vomiting.

This meant no food over the Christmas period. No Christmas dinner. No chocolates. No turkey. Nothing. On this news, my heart broke further. Christmas was my favourite time of year, and the only silver lining had turned grey. I would not be able to enjoy it as much without food.

My coping resilience was low, and this dropped it further. I could not cope with any more hospitals. I could not cope with more tests. I could not cope with any more treatment. I could not cope with any more hope. What makes this surgery any better?

I have had the surgery twice, so why would this work? I had lost control of my life, and people were making plans for my life. I did not want the surgery; I had failed twice, and I didn't want to do that again.

'No, Mum, I don't want the surgery,' I said after she explained the situation.

I did not want it, and for the next two weeks, the house resembled a battlefield. Mum and Dad were telling me I would have it, Sarah hiding away, me having tantrums, no…no way. I was not having it. Mum was telling me that if I don't have it, I would be proving to everyone that I was crazy.

Mum was telling me that she had been watching her child die and that if I didn't have the surgery, the disease would kill me. Mum was using every possible argument to try and get me to change my mind.

My parents told me in no uncertain terms that I would be having the surgery. I had no say. My body was their choice. They were desperate and adamant that I had no choice. I literally had no choice.

Whilst we were waiting for a surgery date. Christmas came and went. Unlike the many years before, it was hard work for everyone involved. We all tried our best. My aunty invited us over for Christmas Day dinner, and it smelled magnificent, and I just sat there watching everyone eat.

I felt numb; it was like I was a ghost at the table. Laughing and joking sailed past me like ships in the night, and I felt out of my body watching from a distance. I was a shell of a person.

My cousins told me a few years later that this meal was really difficult for them, as I was not eating, and that they tried their hardest to be normal, and they were incredible. In our household, we had been used to me; they were not.

Looking back, I was in the midst of such a deep depression. Having to live through all the force-feeding and now being forced into having surgery, I literally felt like it was happening again. I was in constant fight or flight mode. I could not switch it off. I was on edge.

There was no person who had my back who was advocating for what I wanted. I was not allowed to make choices about my body. No one was fighting my battles; in fact, the people who were meant to be fighting my battles were actively forcing me to have this surgery. Our broken relationship was now in tatters. I was completely alone.

* * * *

On 9 January, I was dragged to the hospital. The night before, there was a screaming match between Mum, Dad and me. I did not want the surgery, and Mum was desperate for me to have it.

She kept telling me she didn't want me to die and that this was the only way that would stop it; she was beside herself in desperation. This broke my heart, but I could not understand why, if the first two didn't work, why would this one? More importantly. I could not understand why she could not understand this.

Mum took me to the hospital that morning by public transport, and I dragged my heels all the way. Thinking of ways to get away from her; running away and hiding until after the surgery date. When we got to the hospital, she signed the consent form. I sat there crying.

Next thing I knew, I was going into theatre, tears rolling down my face as my mum was telling me everything would be okay. The only positive about surgery was that I may die.

'Please, God,' I begged.

They put the mask over my face, and I fell asleep.

I woke up in recovery again with Mum next to me.

'Surgery went well, Kayleigh. They did it open.'

I felt like I had been assaulted, both physically and mentally.

'I feel sick,' I said.

The nurse started fussing and gave me medication. I passed out. Waking up later in HDU, it turned out that the cyclizine (anti-sickness) they had given me, I was allergic to, and my blood pressure had plummeted. I was connected to the heart monitors and fentanyl pumps with lots of fluids.

I took the oxygen off my face, and I called out to the nurse, 'I feel sick.' They gave me more medication, but it did not improve. I slipped in and out of my drug-induced haze. Mum and Dad visited, and even Sarah got to visit.

I kept telling the doctors and nurses, 'I feel sick.'

No matter what drugs they gave me, they would not alleviate the symptoms. The surgeon reported that the surgery was difficult because of adhesions; my liver had been stuck to my diaphragm, but other than that, it went well.

It had not gone well, and I felt sick.

Five days later, I was moved onto the teen ward again. I felt too sick to eat, and the smell of food made me retch. I had never felt nausea like this. They kept telling me it would improve, but it wasn't.

I tried to eat, and although I was not sick, I wanted to heave up everything. I retched and retched, and when that had stopped, I curled up into a ball, crying. Why was God punishing me?

Two weeks of this continued, and one morning, the surgeons informed me that I would be going to surgery again. No, no more surgery, when Mum came, she told me that she had already agreed to it. I begged for no more surgery, but Mum ignored my pleas, and the following morning I had a peg inserted.

A peg was a more permanent tube that goes through your abdomen wall into your stomach instead of the NG tube. Mum and Dad had always been dead set against this tube as it was more permanent, and I was going to be cured. Why had they changed their minds? Did they know something I didn't? Have they given up hope?

Mum saw me in and out of the theatre. I said nothing; again, it felt like an assault on my physical and mental health. I did not understand. My parents were siding with the doctors again. I was being forced to have painful procedures. I was left with this awful nausea that was not improving.

Mum and Dad were desperate; they tried everything to get me on board. They were witnessing their daughter slip away before their very eyes. I had been losing weight again, was tired all the time and could not focus. Mum and Dad just hoped that this time it would be my miracle cure.

This time it would work. Whereas I had lost that hope and no longer trusted any adult to make a decision on my behalf, this included my parents. However, because I was under 16, I had no say in my treatment.

As I was recovering from both surgeries, Dad came and visited me. He explained that Newcastle United, the football team we support, were playing at Craven Cottage, down the road from the hospital. He went on to say that he had gotten tickets and was kidnapping me from the hospital for three hours.

Dad was not normally rebellious, but I thought he knew how much I was struggling and wanted to bring a smile to my face. Dad and I had such a lovely time cheering on Newcastle. Dad also enjoyed himself. During half-time, I had to go to the first aider area to give myself a bolus feed as it was due, but it finished before the second half.

The nausea was really uncomfortable, but watching the football was such a great distraction. Unfortunately, Newcastle United did not win that game, but Dad had succeeded in bringing a smile to my face.

This was one of my all-time favourite memories with my dad. I remember one of the Newcastle team injured his crotch and was rolling around holding his manhood right in front of us.

Dad made an attempt to cover my eyes, which made me laugh at him. It wasn't like the player was going wang out his manhood in the middle of the field in front of the fans. When the game finished, we went back to the ward and back to my living nightmare.

I was discharged from the hospital a week later. I was still crippled with nausea; nothing they had done had made me feel better. The fact that I wasn't vomiting was not even joyous, because of the severity of the nausea. Before, I was not allowed to eat. Now I could eat, but didn't want to. I was worse now; I should not have had the surgery.

The second I woke up from the surgery and felt that nausea, I had no idea it was never going to improve. Each day it did not get better was a day my soul sank into a depression. The was no happiness. I felt like I had been assaulted; my brain was processing having major surgery against my will. Not one but two surgeries.

Then one of these surgeries had left you with this unbearable symptom. My relationship with my parents became non-existent. I could not forgive them. Not that they were apologising, they saw the surgery as fixing me, they couldn't see my point of view, and I could not understand their point of view. I was alone again.

* * * *

Home was no longer my safe place. I had my feeds, and I would lie in front of the TV mindlessly, trying to distract myself from the nausea. On days I went to school, mum would have to push me through the front door, crying my eyes out, because I felt so sick.

I felt as though I wanted to vomit constantly, and when I ate and drank, I would get this massive wave of nausea that would cause me to wretch. It was irretractable. It was awful.

Each night I cried into my pillow, I hated God. Why the hell did he do this to me? Why could he be so cruel? I could finally eat without vomiting, and you give me a symptom to stop me from doing that.

What a hateful God. People would tell me, he only gives you things you could cope with, where I was begging every night to die peacefully in my sleep, and he kept failing to afford me that luxury.

By March, mum had paid again for me to be seen by Great Ormond Street, who believed I had an injury to my vagus nerve, which was a big nerve that sends messages from the brain to the heart and gastrointestinal systems. They accepted my case and agreed for me to be seen on the NHS.

They recommended medication, with no improvement and gave the advice to give it time and things should improve. This upset me, time? Is that two weeks or two years? The doctor just said that he was unable to predict, and when I knew, I would know. The hopelessness continued.

Greengate gave up on me, citing that they had done their surgery and that my current symptoms would now need to be followed up by Dr Zhang. The only good thing was that I would never have to see or set foot in that hospital again.

Even now, writing about that hospital or thinking about how they treated me, fills me with sadness and despair. Having been diagnosed with C-PTSD, I have known triggers around being forced into the surgery, my therapeutic relationships with doctors are guarded and difficult, and I feel unable to trust doctors and their advice, as I had seen firsthand that their guidance could make you worse.

Dr Zhang undertook an electrogastrogram (EGG), which was abnormal, and following a barium meal, informed us of a transient hold-up at the GoJ junction. This pretty much meant that food was held up at a point where the food pipe becomes the stomach, where the surgery was, but no other concerns. This would explain why I would struggle to swallow certain foods.

I was in and out of school during this time; it really depended on the symptoms. My head of year asked Mum and me to attend a meeting, and I was a little terrified that I was going to be told off. My brain went straight to I was going to get told off.

I believed that the hospital trauma was now impacting my relationship with all adults who held powerful positions in my life, nurses, doctors, Mum and Dad, and now teachers. I was terrified.

As we sat at reception, my head of year called us through to this very old room filled with wooden panels. Mum updated her with what was happening, although she left the mental health stuff out, which I was thankful for. My head of year just wanted to see if there was anything more they could do to help me and maybe improve my attendance.

The three of us could not think of anything. My head of year also explained that my year was going to go on a school trip abroad, but because I had missed the deadline to say I could go, I would not be able to and instead could come to school and work in the library.

Although what she said made sense, a little bit of me was disappointed, but I understood. It just felt like another thing that this illness had taken away from me.

As the conversation came to a close, we politely said our goodbyes. Mum went off whilst I attended my next lesson.

April happened yet again and turned 14; we marked it with gifts and temporary jolliness. It was just another year of sickness.

By July, I was having a difficult time swallowing and getting food into my stomach without choking or regurgitating. I was yet again bringing up all my food and drink, and now I was left with irretractable nausea, retching, waves of nausea and generalised discomfort.

Dr Zhang planned yet another endoscopy, which showed that the fundoplication was partially unwrapped. I had two small gastric erosions and thickening and inflammation throughout my oesophagus. Due to the symptoms, he took biopsies to establish whether I had any allergies. A few weeks later.

We were informed that it had shown that I had a condition called eosinophilic oesophagitis triggered by a milk allergy. This meant that whilst I was having my milk-based feeds, due to my allergy, my gastrointestinal system was becoming red and raw.

The medication I took for my asthma was increased, and I was told this should improve my symptoms, but there was no improvement.

I believed it was just another coincidental finding. I did not put much hope in this being the curative diagnosis. I just could not do that to myself. The emotional rollercoaster that I had experienced was just too much.

* * * *

Mum was now so fearful that we could end up down the mental health route; she became desperate and started looking at alternative treatments.

At the end of July, Mum took me to a hypnotherapist. She drove me to a red brick house around 40 minutes away, and we knocked at the door of this routine suburban house.

We were met at the door by a flamboyant lady with brown hair and bouncy curls. She ushered me into her house, moving her British bulldog out of the way. She told us that her husband had built an extension on her house for her to do her work.

Mum and I were shown into a room with a couch, where I was asked to lie down. Mum was invited to sit on a single chair. The hypnotist, quite dramatically, sat on a wheelie chair which she moved from her work desk, to face the couch I was lying on.

The room smelt of lavender and incense, one wall was completely filled with bookcases and books, the room had a window with flowing curtains of red and gold, which matched the chair upholstery.

She went through my history in detail, and then she explained that what she could do was put me under hypnosis and introduce stresses, to see what I'd react at, she called it *the emotional freedom technique*.

She told me that I would be in control the whole time, and she placed a heart rate probe on my finger. I don't remember a lot of it, but I remember being told to think of a calm space and thinking of a big lake with trees around it.

I felt super relaxed, like I was floating on a cloud, that was until she brought up doctors, and when she did, I jumped out of the hypnotherapy. I went to apologise to the lady, and I looked over to Mum, who had fallen asleep on the couch.

The lady politely woke up Mum and joked that she should have charged for two. She then informed Mum that, in her opinion, all my issues are physical, but that I have trauma around doctors.

I could have told her that without being hypnotised!

She said she would write a letter for the doctors to see, telling them that I was not mentally ill.

We left the house in a slightly more relaxed state than we got there in, but I was still feeling sick.

My old swimming instructor contacted my mum and told her of this new capsule and gummies that could fix everything. We went to this meeting one Thursday evening at her house, it was full of like-minded people telling Mum how amazing this magic capsule and gummies were.

Mum brought a box full of these expensive gummy bears, which were going to cure me. I had them all, with no improvement.

As an adult, I am sure that was a pyramid scheme and they were preying on vulnerable and desperate people, of which we were both. Looking back now, it angers me how Mum's vulnerability was easy pickings for this lady. She was just seen as a cash cow for a pyramid scheme. Mum was so desperate that she was trying everything.

Mum came home on Thursday and called me downstairs. I got up and meandered my way downstairs as slowly as possible. At the bottom of the stairs, there were two wristbands with a plastic nodule in them.

She explained that these wristbands are for people who experience travel sickness. They work on acupuncture points to help with nausea. I wore them for two weeks constantly, with no improvement.

One of the parents of a primary school friend recommended aloe vera squished into a drink and said it would kill all the inflammation. She drank it regularly and sang its praises.

She filled a cup up for me, and I took the tiniest of sips. It felt so slimy, it was literally my sensory nightmare. I refused to drink any more. I got told off for wasting good aloe vera.

I saw my actions as heroic, less likely for the next person to suffer!

Mum took me to a wellbeing event in the grounds of Crystal Palace (our local football team). We entered, and there were lots of stalls with different types of alternative treatments. We walked past each stall, where possible, we took the leaflets (and any freebies!). Mum was very interested in acupuncture.

She spoke at length to the acupuncturist about my situation. He explained that he would not be able to stab me with needles as I was under 16, but Mum could have a go. Although Mum was a bit disappointed, *I wasn't*. She agreed to it and sat on a chair whilst the gentleman pinged the smallest needles into her ears.

I stood there watching, but it was not that interesting to watch. Afterwards, Mum tried to tell me that it was very relaxing as we left the event. I don't know whether I believed her, but bless her for trying.

Mum found the homoeopathic hospital in London and we started going there every Tuesday for Reiki therapy. It was nice to lie down and deep breathe, whilst people fussed over you. After the first session, they referred to my stomach as being *spaghetti junction*. Mum absorbed it as though it meant something.

The logical part of my brain thought that we told you the issue was my stomach and that it would have been more impressive if we didn't tell you what the issue was, and you found it out. But at this point, we were desperate and trying everything to make mum happy, so I went for the six sessions.

Each session, I would lie on a bed and the practitioner would wave her hands up and down my body, close enough that I could feel the heat radiating off her hands but not touching.

At first, it was awkward, but after a while, that went away, and the hardest bit was sitting still for the 40 minutes. I remember that the waiting room had quotes from all the famous people who had attended.

I couldn't remember most, but one of Trinny and Susanna had used it, although I'm not sure which one! Unfortunately, there was no improvement, although I am not surprised; there were some unexpected benefits.

Going to this place once a week for six weeks and having 40 minutes unplugged from my phone or the TV was really difficult; being left with my own thoughts was terrifying, but as the weeks went on, it became easier.

The second unexpected benefit was that the time that Mum and I started spending with each other, travelling into London and back, was really healing for us. It was a couple of hours of no arguing and actual chatting. A few times, we also went to the theatre too, it was a really bonding time, something mum and I really needed.

* * * *

Sarah and I were sitting, watching TV. Mum and Dad came into the room and informed us that we would be travelling to Lourdes as part of a pilgrimage, connected to the church. Sarah would be missing her final day in primary school and her school party.

Lourdes was a pilgrimage, one of the holiest pilgrimages for Catholics. The story is that the Virgin Mary visited a 14-year-old peasant girl called Bernadette. She had 18 encounters with the Virgin Mary. On Wikipedia, it said that Lourdes had special appeal for the fragile and weak.

Really love the word weak for us. It's a great word for disabled people—some of the strongest people I know.

So early on 21 July, we piled onto a coach, en route to Lourdes. I remember the date as it was the same day the final Harry Potter book came out. Two people in our pilgrimage group had come a day late and had brought the book at the airport.

I was so jealous!

The journey went off to a rocky start as my area was having a lot of storms, and a local underpass got flooded. This had gotten into all the local papers, and it felt like we were leaving chaos. It didn't really affect us as we were going via the Channel Tunnel. *Which, if I thought about it, was just a big underpass—luckily it didn't flood!*

We were a group of 30ish people, some disabled, some carers and some just family. There was a priest as part of our group, and we stayed in a place called Hallelujah House, which was a specially adapted house for disabled people and had a chapel connected to it. Meals were catered for—not that I needed it, but this felt like a little holiday.

The group was filled with people I knew and some I didn't. Sarah had some people her age there, but there was no one my age, so I would either hang out with the adults or with the children. They gave us little jobs to do, to help us integrate into the group as well.

On our first day, we went on a pilgrimage walk. When we got to the holy shrine, my mum dosed me in the water, like she was putting out a fire. She had been given a list of people, including my grandma, who wanted her to bring back holy water, so we were scooping it up in reusable water bottles.

We were travelling back through the Channel Tunnel, so there were no 100 mL limitations that you get on the aeroplanes, so we could bring home bottles and bottles of it for the relatives.

The shrine itself was not really interesting to look at; you could only look into it and reach the fountain. It had the Virgin Mary overlooking it and lots of candles. Following the pilgrimage walk, we went to the church that was built by the shrine and participated in an English-speaking mass. This church was the biggest I had ever seen. It...was...huge.

At Hallelujah House, they had organised lots of activities, competitions and masses, that everyone was invited to attend, irrespective of their additional needs or no needs. It was so lovely to be involved in things, as since my health had deteriorated, I had again been sidelined from everything.

It had felt like I was looking at life through a window, but this place allowed me to be present. The activities were not all God based, so it didn't feel like we were at church. We had a theme which was butterflies, animals that are resilient and delicate at the same time, and a number of activities were butterfly-based.

We also scattered the ashes of people who had requested this, prior to their deaths, *obviously*. We did have a slight hiccup; we all stood downwind of the people scattering the ash, and with one big gust of wind, we all got a good mouthful of the ash.

Mmm, human charcoal—tasty!

One day, we went up into the mountains and spent the day swimming in pools and by a huge, beautiful lake. It was a cloudy but warm day, and my Celtic skin burnt under the French mountain sun (even with factor 50 sun lotion). We had a game of water volleyball against another pilgrim group as well, which was fun.

I couldn't remember who won, but I loved every minute of it. It was nice to feel normal even if it was only for a week. By removing my family from the dire situation at home, we got on better and argued less, which was nice too.

One night, Mum came to me and asked if I would go with the group and submerge in the holy water. I asked if I could do it in my swimming costume, and she informed me that I would have to be naked, but it was all above board. No one would see anything.

Not in 100 years was I getting naked in front of strangers. No and no again. 100% no. The idea of 14-year-old me doing this even now makes me squirm inside. I was a prude, and not European in that sense. I know Mum was disappointed, and she did her best to try and persuade me, but it wasn't going to happen.

Even now, that would be a nope! Also, Moses in the Bible got to wear clothes during baptism, why do they need nakedness now? Catholicism is quite a conservative religion, whereas nakedness is much more liberal. Not that I believe I am a kin to Moses, although we have both climbed mountains, he Mount Sinai, and I, Ben Nevis!

We left the next day and returned home to a soggy UK. The floods had receded, but the UK just looked a bit sad compared to sunny France.

No miracle for me. My symptoms never changed.

I have found myself wondering if I had dipped in that holy water, would I be cured? If the real reason I was not cured was because I did not Jesus hard enough?

* * * *

The regurgitation and nausea continued. The nausea was split into two: constant background nausea and waves of nausea. The waves of nausea would cause retching, but I had had the waves of nausea for years, and the constant nausea had been present since the surgery. I was fatigued as I was not tolerating enough feed to sustain me.

I was not eating because of the nausea; I had to skip meals just to function. I was losing weight, and I was not sleeping well because of the nausea. I wanted the surgery out of me, and next time I saw Dr Zhang, I begged for it to be removed; however, this was refused.

I had returned to school in year 10, when it had reopened after the summer holiday. My uniform was loose on me. My fatigue was high. This was the start of my GCSE year, so I felt the normal pressures on my shoulders of my GCSEs, and I wanted so much to be there.

I still didn't have friends to hang out with, but I had people who were friendly with me, so I bounced between people. Since my schooling had been so hit and miss in the previous years, I had dropped sets, so everyone around me was new. I had to build new relationships, which was something I did find hard.

One girl referred to me as being the new girl as she had never seen me before, it was only the fourth or fifth time of calling me that, I explained that I had been in her year since year seven. She refused to believe me, but it was only until other people backed up my story, she apologised. I had also dropped classes like French, as I had missed too much to catch up now. My illness prevailed.

I could cope with vomiting, but not the nausea. It was interfering with every moment of every day. Every happiness was tinged with nausea. My body had started going into starvation mode, and on 14 September, I was admitted to the hospital.

I was in Elephant Bay again, in the bed opposite where I had been before, but still by the window. The first thing they trialled was a different anti-sickness. It would help the waves of nausea, but not the constant nausea or vice versa.

They trialled me on mental health medication as it could help with the gut/brain systems—no improvement. They trialled me with medication they give to cancer patients, with no improvement.

They would be measuring what was going into me and what was coming out, and it was literally five mL in five mL out. I was unable to cope with anything more than 40 mL an hour before I was incapacitated with nausea.

I shared my bay with Brodie, who was back in again, an 18-month-old boy called Jake and a 14-year-old girl called Harriet.

Jake's mum was called Carol, and his dad was called Pete. Carol told me that he was a happy and healthy little boy hitting all the usual milestones, until he wasn't and he started regressing. He soon stopped talking and walking, and crawling.

Carol had dark brown hair, which Jake had also inherited in the gene pool, although he had Pete's eyes. Carol was so sweet, I could hold conversations with her, and she never made me feel like I was a child.

Harriet was 14, and she had a condition called anorexia nervosa. She was very skinny and looked unwell. Her mum was a little Malaysian mum who tried her hardest to feed her.

As the days melted into weeks, Brodie left, and a boy called Liam came. He had a condition called Crohn's, and he was 15 years old. He was allowed to smoke because it helped him manage his symptoms. He was on something called total parenteral nutrition, a bag of feed would go into a line, which went into his heart because his bowel didn't absorb nutrition.

* * * *

Dr Zhang had not given up on me; each evening, he would come to my bedside with a new test or a repeat test.

I remember there was one time, he connected me to an electrogastrogram or EGG test where they put electrodes on my stomach and I had to lie still for an hour or two. He did this test on me for four days in a row.

On the fourth day, he did not come back at the two-hour mark, like he had the three other times. By the fourth hour, I was desperate for the toilet, and the nurses called his mobile.

It turned out that he was called at home. He had forgotten he had hooked me up to the machine and went home for dinner at the end of the day. The results came back abnormal, but the results did not confirm what the issues were.

Dr Zhang even used herbal Chinese traditional medicine with no improvement. Ginger, peppermint, lemon and even pressure points.

Each day I was there, my cannula would tissue, where it comes out of the vein, and the fluid starts seeping into the surrounding tissue. Due to this, I would need a new one. However, it was becoming increasingly difficult to site a cannula as my veins were so scarred from having four years of cannulations.

It would now take two or three people to try before an anaesthetist was called, all because my veins were so bad. Although a cannula is just as sharp as a scratch, when you're having back-to-back tries, it builds up.

I knew I had to stay still, but your body wants to pull itself away because it's in pain; you are literally fighting against natural protective urges. I used to cope by imagining a big barrier coming up between me and the needle, which stopped me from pulling away, and I sat calmly through the pain.

The coping mechanism was some form of dissociative behaviour where I managed to get through these symptoms; I was almost out of my own body. There were moments when I was going through procedures as simple as a blood test, and I felt like the big barrier came up and that the pain was on one side of the barrier and that I was on the other side of the barrier and no longer in my body.

I still feel the pain, but somehow it was less, or maybe it allowed me to cope with it more. It's probably not that healthy, but it got me through hospital tests, investigations and triggers. It's less helpful in day-to-day life, where it could be triggered by something inane, and suddenly I dissociate.

Each day, the teacher would pop his head in, and I would not see him the rest of the day. That was my education.

I stopped eating because of the nausea. It was just too much eating and then feeding, and the nausea was just impenetrable. When the doctors realised this and they told the nurses that I needed to try. At dinner time, they would bring a trolley around, and the nurse told me I had to eat.

I refused, she told me that no was not an option. They also had a habit of trying to increase my feed without me noticing. The issue was that I would start retching and could not understand why, before the feed rate was pointed out.

I thought the word I would use now was triggered. I was completely triggered by North Surrey Hospital. It was like I was reliving that awful treatment again.

I burst into tears. I was not sure why this was the catalyst, but once the tear train started rolling. It did not stop. I hysterically cried, four years' worth of bad treatment and trauma. The emotion exited my soul through my tear ducts that day. I was inconsolable. That evening, the nurses moved me to the Monkey Bay.

The staff were concerned that Harriet and her anorexia nervosa were rubbing off on me. The following morning, the mum of this girl came to me and begged me to choose not to be like her daughter. I tried to tell her I wasn't trying to be like her daughter, but the more I argued, the more she didn't believed me.

This made me more anxious; I was worried the nurses would think I was crazy because of the tears. I refused to have the feed overnight as I had lost trust in the medical staff to not change my feed rate.

Whereas, in reality, I was going through a hard time. Crying when you are going through difficulty is a normal reaction. I was made to feel that my crying was a sign of mental weakness, so I had to just cope. Even to this day, I find crying really triggering for me; my brain sees it as a last resort or crisis. It was a catalyst for all the bad memories.

On 4 October, I underwent a further endoscopy, which showed ongoing eosinophilic oesophagitis *damn.* During this endoscopy. Dr Zhang decided to use my peg and place a tube through it. The end of this tube would be further down into my bowel. It was known as a GJ tube.

The hope was that if it was not going into my stomach, my symptoms would improve. The doctors also contacted Greengate to request a reversal of my surgery. They refused.

By the end of October, I had lost five kg, despite being admitted to the hospital. Great Ormond Street recommended a much stronger steroid course for the eosinophilic oesophagitis and to wait and see if there was any improvement.

The GJ tube, which had been placed, did not help with the nausea; in fact, it made the waves of nausea worse. On occasion, I would be crippled with my nausea, and after two days of the doctors downplaying my nausea, they decided to see where the tube was.

It had, in fact, migrated up to my stomach, which would be why the nausea was so bad. It took two hours to be replaced in radiology.

I had been moved to a side room after an outbreak of diarrhoea and vomiting on the children's ward. I was lucky that I didn't become unwell.

The anorexic girl went to a specialist hospital, and her bed was taken by an equally thin girl, called Alice. Unlike Harriet, she would eat, though, but could only have one or two bites before she was full. Jake stayed in his bed, and I would poke my head around when I could and was allowed. The bed that I had been in was full of short-term patients, and Liam was soon discharged.

I started the treatment three weeks later, and the doctors decided that I was to be discharged because I would hopefully thrive at home. So, on 31 October, Halloween night, Mum picked me up and I returned to the house, where Sarah's friends from high school had come over for Halloween.

* * * *

In our house, we did not celebrate Halloween, as being a Catholic, it was frowned upon, but as we got older, we liked dressing up. Mum point-blank refused to let us go begging our neighbours for sweets, but did allow us to have a few people over. This had stopped whilst I had been sick, but Sarah wanted it so badly that Mum had agreed. Just some normality.

I said hello to everyone, but I was exhausted and took myself to bed quite early. Happiness did not feel like an emotion I deserved at that time. I didn't know what the future would hold, and I was feeling it weigh heavy on my chest. It was like I was suffocating.

Each day I took the medication. Each day I had the feed. Each day, I was more and more tired. One morning, I had a bath and felt so ill that I had to remove myself from the bath to lie on the floor. I looked up at the ceiling and cried. Was this my life?

Each day, I was more and more dehydrated, and four days later, mum told me she was taking me back to the hospital. I was too tired to even fight it. I numbly packed my bag, and I was taken to the hospital by car.

When I got to A&E, I was rushed through and when they saw my bloods, my kidneys were affected by the dehydration. Dr Zhang referred to me as being a prune. He was not someone to be dramatic, so I must have been. They hooked me up to IV fluids, and each drop made me feel better. I must have slept for 20 hours straight. I was placed in Monkey Bay again, but in a different bed.

The next morning, the doctors informed me that GOSH was going to admit me for tests, but until then, they were going to continue with what they were doing.

Jake was discharged to a hospice, and I was moved into his space. I waved Carol and Jake off I knew what a hospice was, but I was not fully aware of what that actually meant. In the four days I had been away, Brodie was back, and it was nice to catch up with Sue and our postman.

They did not stay long before she was discharged. Alice was diagnosed with superior mesenteric artery (SMA) syndrome and discharged home. Liam had been back and gone again. Alice and Liam had made friends, which was nice. We gave each other our emails and numbers to stay in contact.

We followed each other on Facebook, and I bumped into Alice one day whilst walking around Epsom. Alice went on to study art and then accountancy. She was a fantastic artist. Alice continued to live with her disease, but she enjoyed cooking and posted a lot about food.

Liam went on to look after animals, especially budgies, which became his life's worth. He used to talk about his animas so much in the hospital. He unfortunately passed away in his 30s from complications with Crohn's in 2024. I credit Liam with my life, which I explain later in the book.

Other than the regular CF patients and the others I have mentioned, life on the ward was mundane. The patients flit in and out each day; some stayed a few days, others one or two, but they all went home.

For me, they were trying to build up my feed tolerance, but unfortunately, I was struggling to get past 40 mLsls per hour before the nausea was too much. The nausea would wake me up, so I would have the feed during the day. I was losing weight rapidly, and they started weighing me daily.

There was a lot of pressure around weighing; the doctors would make a big thing about the weight loss, and I had no idea what I was meant to be. Some of the staff started becoming difficult with me, as if I was not trying hard enough. I soon started dreading being weight. Each morning before my feed came, I would feel anxiety in the pit of my stomach.

On top of this, my cannula was tissuing two to three times a day, and vein access was near impossible, even the self-proclaimed *line king* failed, with ultrasound. Anaesthetists would be asked to come up and struggle.

Sometimes they would wheel me to A&E to get one of the doctors there to do it. My tolerance was little, each night I lay looking at the ceiling, wishing I was somewhere else, anywhere else.

* * * *

Each day would consist of waking up. Toilet, weight, discussion about weight loss, and feed. Doctor's round, teacher said hi, play on laptop, Mum visit after her work. Then, Dad visit in the evening, stop the feeding, laptop and bed. With IV fluid throughout, and then somewhere in this boring amalgamation would be two cannula and multiple tries.

By the beginning of November, it was no longer two or three tries but 16 or 17 tries. I would have tears coming down my face, but they would have to continue because I needed the fluid. It was happening so often that I may as well move to the treatment room.

It had been nine days of this on the trot, and I was hitting a brick wall. My cannula had tissued for the second time in the day. It was evening, and we had all been put to bed. I did not feel like I could cope with another round of stabbing, in my arms, wrists, legs, neck, feet and face. I was resembling a sponge with all the holes in me.

I felt overwhelmed. I didn't want to do it again. I needed to get away. I was in fight or flight, and my brain was telling me to flight; go find somewhere safe. I just needed to get away. I needed to be somewhere else. I just wanted a break.

I got myself up and walked down to the playroom, and I fit through the gap in the doors that had been chained up, lying on a big bean bag. I did consider running away from the ward, but I did not want to get into trouble. I was in a bit of a state, just completely overwhelmed.

The playroom was probably the most recently painted in the whole of the children's ward, painted by students whose names were on the wall. It was under a sea theme, and they had incorporated the cupboards and drawers into their paintings too.

I dozed a little on the bean bag, and I woke up to hear my name being called. My heart wanted to respond, but I could not get my brain to settle; there was no reasonable thought process. I thought to myself that they could miss me for a few minutes, and I dozed off.

I woke back up a few minutes later, hearing the nurses talk among themselves.

'We are going to have to call the police and inform her parents,' one said.

'Does anyone know what she was wearing?' said another. 'It's only been an hour, let's give Kayleigh a few more minutes. She may come back.'

F@#k.

I heard the nurses agree and then walk away from where they were standing. They were a fair bit down the ward, just the halls echoed noise, which was why I could hear so clearly. I jumped up from my bean bag, a little too fast that my head spun, which was normal for me.

I snuck back through the chained doors and tried to walk to the other end of the ward, where my bed was. As I did this, one of the nurses caught me.

'Where have you been? We were getting worried.'

'I didn't mean to worry anyone, I just wanted to be by myself.'

'Where were you?'

I didn't answer.

'Where were you?'

'The play room.'

She looked me up and down and informed me that the doctor was going to come later for the cannula, so I should try and sleep.

I dragged myself into bed and cried myself to sleep until I was woken up at 2 am for the cannula. The next night, the playroom was padlocked shut.

* * * *

Brodie was discharged. The CF kids were constantly revolving. They had the side rooms and tended to keep themselves to themselves. Although one or two recognised me as a revolving door patient like them and we soon greeted each other like old friends.

One day myself and one of the other kids, named Shannon, managed to get our hands on 60 mL syringes. As kids do, we filled them up with water and ran after each other, trying to squirt one another, whilst hiding from the nurses.

In these mere minutes, I felt like I was just being a kid again. It was so nice. I laughed for the first time in ages. I felt carefree and happy, but still nauseous.

Our fun came to a halt when a nurse saw what we were doing and took the syringes from us.

She turned to me and said in a tone of disappointment, 'You're meant to be sick.'

I went back to my bed with my tail between my legs, trying to process what that meant. Being sick didn't mean I was not a kid; I was only 14.

I spent the evening worrying that because I didn't behave like I was a sick kid, they were going to believe I was faking everything and go down the mental health route again. I made a promise to myself that I was not going to smile again whilst I was in the hospital. So that the nurses could see that I was a serious patient.

Looking back, I had been so traumatised by the treatment I had experienced in the past, I would do anything to stop it happening again. Even if I never experienced happiness again, it was a risk I was willing to take.

* * * *

I had a tube going into my stomach called a PEG tube. Inside this tube, I had a second tube that went into the part of the bowel called the Jejunum. The combination of the two tubes was called a GJ tube.

The reason I had the second tube was to bypass the stomach with the hope that my symptoms would improve. Although they were better, I still struggled to have a feed rate of more than 40 mL an hour without the nausea being unmanageable alongside retching and vomiting.

My bowel tube also had a nasty habit of going back up into my stomach, and my symptoms would worsen. I would be taken down to interventional radiology, where they would try and thread it back into my bowel. Which could take hours, and it was difficult.

I could see Dr Zhang got more and more frustrated at it, not wanting to stay where it was meant to be. I vividly remember the radiologist tapped my abdomen with a wooden spoon a number of times to stimulate my stomach to keep the tube in the right place. It didn't work.

It was mid-November. I had lost 10 kg in a month. My clothes were loose on me. Mum had to downsize my pyjamas. Alice's mum came to the ward on Thursday afternoon to pick something up for her daughter. I was standing chatting to one of the nurses by the entrance. Alice's mum came through the door and looked at me,

'My God, you now look worse than Alice.'

I didn't really know how to respond to this comment. Alice looked like a skeleton: did I truly look like her?

Next time I used the bathroom, I stood at the sink and really looked at myself in the mirror above it. I had big rings around my sunken eyes. My skin was pale and dry. My once plumped cheekbones were now skeletal.

I lifted up my top to expose my belly and saw my ribs protruding through my skin with a concave abdomen. My hip bones stuck out, and my once-tight leggings rippled on my legs from the weight loss. I looked awful.

The following morning, I was having my daily weight done, and the nurses were making a fuss about the amount of weight I had lost in a day, as if I were doing it on purpose. I had started experiencing a lot of anxiety around these daily weights, but I told no one.

Due to how awful this was, I struggle to weigh myself as an adult. It was a trigger for my C-PTSD and anxiety.

I was having the peg feed low overnight. However, the nurses started changing the rate when I was asleep, and I would wake up retching. It was horrible.

I refused to have the feed overnight anymore and would only have it in the day, at least then I know that the staff would not be able to try and trick me into more feed because it had not been working and I was getting ill. *This also became a CPTSD trigger.*

Dr Zhang was the consultant undertaking the ward rounds and just happened to be passing by when the nursing staff were having their daily weight complaint.

'Kayleigh, we need to do something about this weight loss. You do not have any safe fat to lose anymore, and you will start losing muscle mass, including from your heart.'

'Do you remember Liam? He had that thing called total parenteral nutrition (TPN), which helped him keep his weight level right.'

I didn't wait for him to respond and asked, 'Can I have that?'

I knew how much it helped Liam when he had lost weight. I wanted that. I was tired all the time, I was being weighed daily, and it was worrying me. I was in no man's land and getting weaker and weaker. Dr Zhang was initially shocked by my question, but he went away to think about it.

The following day, he called Mum on the phone and discussed TPN. Between him, Dad and Mum, they agreed that this was an important step to keep my weight stable, whilst we were waiting for the Great Ormond Street admission. The ball started to get rolling.

I was informed on the following doctor's round that I was going to have a Hickman line (a catheter placed in the big blood vessels in my chest), placed in the theatre, tomorrow. Following this, I would be given TPN, which was a bag of calories, vitamins and nutrients.

The next day was a buzz of excitement, not because of the TPN, but because footballers from the local team were coming into the hospital to meet the sick kids. It was exciting, but I was worried they were going to come as I was being taken down to the theatres.

I sat expectedly, in a hospital gown all day, waiting to be called for theatres. I was in a good mood because I was nil by PEG-J and the nausea was bearable.

At lunchtime, the chatting on the ward intensified as three of the players came onto the ward. They started in Monkey Bay and worked their way through the other bay, at which point they reached me.

They spoke to me about why I was there, how long I had been in the hospital for, three months at this point. I told them about today's procedure, and they politely listened and wished me well.

The photographer who came with them took a photo of us together, and they moved on to the next patient. Within 10 minutes of speaking to them, the porter came up to take me to the theatres.

That photo got into the local newspaper, although they spelt my name hideously!

I was taken into the anaesthetic room, where I assumed they were going to put me to sleep. It was at this moment, I was informed I would be having the procedure awake, without any sedation, just reliant on local anaesthetic. I thought to myself, it couldn't be that bad if I was having it awake.

They confirmed who I was and the procedure I was to have; they then hooked me up to the cardiac monitor and blood pressure machine and wheeled me into the theatre. I remember feeling really nervous, and I held onto the side rail attached to my bed, my knuckles white with fear.

There were two people in the room, both covered up in their blue scrub outfits, wearing masks, so I could only see their eyes.

One of the doctors was in his 60s, he had blue eyes and glasses, and you could see wisps of white hair poking out from his scrub hat. The second doctor was younger; he was East Asian looking with brown eyes. They obviously had a good rapport with each other as they were chatting away.

This was probably the first time in my life that I was in a room with only men that I didn't know. It was a very vulnerable position to be in.

They explained that they would need to clean my chest with an antimicrobial to make sure no bugs infect the position. The Asian doctor pulled down the sheet, exposing my breast. I looked up at the ceiling and held onto the bedside even tighter.

After cleaning the area, I attempted to cover myself, but the doctor stopped me and said that he would put a drape over me to cover me up. I felt completely vulnerable and embarrassed as I lay there whilst the doctors were sorting things out.

It felt like too long, but I was eventually covered up. Both doctors did try to chat to me, but I was not having any of it; I felt too awkward.

Once covered, they explained they would be injecting local anaesthetic into my chest.

'This will feel like a bee sting,' the grey-haired doctor said as he poked me with a needle, and I felt a sharp stinging pain in my chest.

He did it again and again, and finally said, 'All done, that's the worst of it.'

It was not like a bee sting at all; in fact, much worse. *I thought they say that so they don't feel as bad knowing it was uncomfortable.*

He poked the area he had just put local anaesthetic in. I felt a sharp prod and told him that.

He looked at me and said, 'I'll give it a minute.'

He probably waited 30 seconds before asking me if I could feel it, and again I said I could.

'Okay, well, it's normal to feel pressure,' he responded and commenced the procedure.

I lay still as I felt the doctor cut into my chest, I felt every swipe of the blade, the cut they placed in my neck. I felt the moment they stabbed through my chest, connecting the exit site with the neck cut. I felt every stitch. I could not move out of fear, and the doctor had said it's okay. Maybe I was just not good with pain.

Was I a baby? Why does it hurt so bad? My eyes filled with tears, and my hand was cramping as I continued to white knuckle the bedside. I felt dizzy during the procedure and told the doctors, and they momentarily stopped as I composed myself before they continued the procedure. The procedure lasted around 20 minutes.

As the doctor told me, it was the last stitch. I took a big breath. My chest felt like it was on fire. I wiped the tears and thanked the two doctors as they removed all the drapes, exposing my breasts again. I went to cover myself up, but this time I was not stopped.

In my later years, I found out that local anaesthetic does not work on me and because of this, I went through this procedure feeling everything.

I was taken back to the ward. All of the excitement from the footballers had gone, and the ward had returned to normal. It was the evening now, and some of the bays were being put to bed.

I closed the curtains around my bed and gingerly put my pyjamas on. I got under the blanket, and as my head hit the pillow, I cried. It wasn't the last time I would cry myself to sleep.

* * * *

We got a new boy in our bay. He came in in the early hours of the morning. In the morning, he introduced himself to the room.

'Hello, I am Zak.'

We started chatting and I found out that he was a year older than me, and he was admitted for cellulitis. He was bitten by a spider, and the wound got infected.

I had my daily weight and had started my feed. During the doctor's round, they told him they would give him one dose of IV antibiotics, then switch him to oral antibiotics, and he could go home. Even though he was not here long, it was nice to speak to someone my age.

As he left, he handed me a note with his number on it. I felt a girly bubble in the pit of my stomach. He liked me. It was the first time a guy had ever given me his number. I bet I was the last person in my year whom this has happened to.

I was very excited and added his number to my phone, although I was not going to text straight away. I don't want to look too eager.

After the doctor's round, the dietitian came to me. She sat down, so I knew it was going to be a long one. She explained that although I had been having some nutrition, it hadn't been enough to sustain me and that I likely have not had adequate nutrition for a long time.

She explained that the TPN would be 12 hours overnight, but initially it would start at 24 hours and be slowly ramped up to ensure we flood my body with nutrition, and it does not become overwhelmed and unable to cope, called refeeding syndrome.

She explained that we would go from 24 hours to 12 hours over the next week and undertake regular bloods to make sure everything was okay.

I later found out that in the concentration camps in Nazi Germany, when they were being liberated. After days, months and years of limited nutrition, aid workers would give the freed prisoners food, and as a result, many people died as their bodies were overwhelmed. This was refeeding syndrome.

One of the nurses connected me up to the TPN, and this day felt like every other.

At around 6 pm, after dinner, I had decided that I had waited long enough to text Zac and wrote him a quick message.

'It was nice to meet you, Kayleigh x.'

I quickly pressed send, so I would not overthink it and put the phone down.

I was still in my day top. I hadn't realised I would be unable to disconnect the TPN. So annoyingly, it looked like I would be sleeping in it.

I went to the bathroom and washed my face, and brushed my teeth.

Jake had returned to the hospital, so I went and said hello and spent a little time chatting with Carol. Jake had just celebrated his second birthday, and his dad had brought him a huge toy parrot that would mimic the noises he made. His mum, Carol, was delighted that he was interacting with something.

He now had a tube in his nose as he was unable to eat any more. I looked into the crib and saw his big, beautiful brown eyes through me. Carol said they were going home tomorrow, now that he had the tube. I gave them all my best wishes and left to go to my bay and bed, dragging my IV pole behind me.

I sat on my bed and got under my duvet. When mum visited me today, she brought me my duvet from home, with the hope I would sleep better. I was very excited to go to bed tonight.

I picked my phone up to text Mum and Dad goodnight. I saw that I had a missed call with a voicemail from Zac's number. With butterflies in my stomach, I went to listen to the voicemail.

A gruff, aggressive voice was on the other end of the phone, which didn't sound like the boy; it sounded like an older man, maybe his dad.

I replayed the voice message as I had been taken by surprise and hadn't listened to the words.

'Cunt, stay the fuck away from my son. Don't call, don't text, or you will have me to deal with.'

The phone dropped out of my hand and onto my bed. I was shocked. My hand was shaking and I burst into tears. Taking deep breaths, I picked up the phone to delete the message and number. The curtain moved suddenly, and I jumped. It was the nurse looking after me that night. She looked at me and asked if I was okay. I explained what happened and gave her the phone to listen to.

She told me flatly, 'Well, this is what happens when you give your number away.'

As though it was my fault.

Looking back now, a boy asking for a girl's number was a rite of passage in your teenage years. For me, it was more than that. I was skin and bone, but that boy wanted to stay in contact with me; it meant something. I was left to deal with an adult situation on my own. I was humiliated and also a little scared.

When the nurse left my bedside, I deleted his number. Good riddance.

* * * *

Over the next week, we cycled the TPN down to 12 hours overnight. I would still have to feed during the day when the tube worked. I was eating and vomiting and still feeling very nauseous.

1 December came, and the ward was allowed to put Christmas decorations up. The ward was a buzz with excitement. This year, the hospital had been chosen by Harrods to have their leftover/last year's Christmas decorations.

All of the staff participated in putting the decorations up, from the housekeeper to the doctors. It almost felt like Christmas Day watching the staff open the delivery to see what was there.

Soon, each window had an adornment on it in red or gold. The Christmas tree by the nurse's desk was lit up and had red and gold baubles on it with red and gold tinsel. The ward doors were decorated with tinsel and had window stickers saying Merry Christmas. They played Christmas music, and the ward felt a little lighter.

Some of the student nurses even decorated themselves with the leftovers, Christmas hats, tinsel in their hair or on their name badges, and some of the other staff joined in too.

The play specialist brought out the make-your-own decorations, and I spent the day sitting on my bed, feeling very nauseous due to the feed, but being mentally stimulated with this craft.

The doctors have spoken with Mum and Dad about giving me day release. My PEG-J feed could be carried in a backpack, and I could go home for the day, coming back in the evening for TPN. I loved this plan.

The following day, I woke up, disconnected my TPN, had my daily weight, and then put my portable feed up. The teacher said hello, made my bed, and Mum picked me up and drove me home.

She would then go off to work, leaving me at home with Dad, who was working in his office. His employer gave him the flexibility to work from home due to our family's needs, which was nice. Although some days he did have to go into work.

I loved being at home; being home just made me happier. I literally went from hospital bed to home couch and have nice baths, I was still connected to my feed and would need to carry it around. However, the nausea I would feel made just participating in life very hard.

I felt like I could not focus, like I was constantly uncomfortable in my own skin, but this was what the doctors and I agreed on. I was the type of person who kept her word, even if it was hard.

As the days turned to weeks, this was our routine. Sarah soon joined me on the couch as school was off for the winter holiday. We would watch back-to-back Hallmark movies whilst sharing her duvet that she brought downstairs.

She would have her seat, I would have my seat, and we would rot away together. During this time, there were glimmers of normal life existing in a world full of chaos and uncertainty, and we enjoyed the moment, just ignoring the feed that I was connected to and the vomit bowl by my feet.

One Thursday afternoon, Sarah and I were engulfed in a Christmas movie when the ad break commenced. I asked Sarah if she would be kind enough to get me a drink, as it was more difficult for me with my tubes and wires. To my pleasant surprise, she said yes.

Sarah would like the reader to appreciate what a good sister she was being.

She pulled the duvet up and went to stand up when she let out a scream like she had witnessed someone being murdered. The living room door flew open as Mum and Dad sprinted into the room to see what had happened.

Sarah did not move a muscle. She then retched. She pointed to her bare foot. As Mum, Dad and I followed her gaze, we saw what the issue was. We saw it. She has put her foot into my fairly full vomit bowl.

'It's in-between my toes,' she cried as I burst out laughing. She retched again. 'It's still warm!' she whimpered.

'Don't move,' gasped Mum in-between stifled laughs. 'I don't want you to get it on my carpet!'

Sarah looked at Mum with a look that said *You have got to be kidding me.*

Mum went into the kitchen to get a towel as Sarah stood still.

'Ewwwwww,' she just kept repeating, 'ew…ew…ew—'

I was laughing so hard that I was unable to breathe for words. Dad had left the room retching. Mum and Sarah slowly prised her foot out of the gelatinous mess and placed her foot on the towel, wiping away the liquid remnants. She then hopped upstairs to run her foot under the shower, twice.

Mum advised me to move my vomit bowl. I went and emptied it in the loo and moved it away from Sarah. For the rest of the evening, I would burst into fits of giggles as my brain relived the scene I had just witnessed, whilst Sarah told me to shut up with a smile.

* * * *

A week had passed from the vomit bowl incident. Sarah and I were in literally the same positions (although the vomit bowl had moved homes). Today, I felt particularly rubbish. Mum came into the living room and said it was time to go back to the ward.

'Nooo, please another five minutes, Muuuum, please!' I begged.

'Sorry, Kayleigh, it's time,' she responded as her heart broke too.

We had got into a habit of me begging to stay a little longer and Mum saying no. There had been tears, there had been tantrums, and I just didn't want to go back to the ward, but today, I did not have the energy. I shoved all my stuff into my backpack and got into the car.

The drive home was the same, but it was nice seeing that people had started putting their Christmas lights up outside, so we made a game of rating the decorations. I would have loved to have outside decorations at our house, but a mixture of Dad's fear of heights and Mum's fear of not wanting to spend money on silly things meant we missed out.

Dad, Mum and I arrived outside the hospital, and Mum dropped us off. She was going to drive home and spend time with Sarah. She kissed me goodbye and drove away. Dad and

I chatted for a little bit, and the nurse came with my TPN and hooked me up, disconnected my Peg-J-tube.

About 15 minutes later, I started to feel really weird. This complete and utter feeling of doom, like something catastrophic was going to happen imminently. At the same time, I also started feeling really dizzy. I sat up in my bed and felt like the world went blank. The next thing I knew, I was lying down with my head at the foot of my bed.

'Did I just faint?' I said to Dad, but Dad had been looking at a book.

He looked up at me, bemused; he had not seen a thing. I looked up the ward and saw my nurse for the day walking down the hall.

'Did I just faint?' I called out to her.

It felt like my heart was racing.

She looked at me, confused.

'I feel weird,' I said.

She looked at me as though she didn't believe me, but she went and got an observation machine. I asked Dad to pass me my dressing gown as I was feeling really, really cold.

She checked my temperature, then she checked my pulse and blood pressure.

'Kayleigh, you have a fever, you need to take all that off,' she said. 'I am going to get the doctor.'

I looked up at her, like, *f*ck, was I taking all these layers off*? It was freezing. My legs and arms were shivering. I was so cold. I was not going to make that worse. The sense of doom continued, and my heart raced.

The doctors came very quickly, some doctors I recognised, and some I didn't. Some were wearing scrubs, and some were wearing normal clothes. They all looked concerned as they fussed over me. I felt really weird.

They asked my dad to sit in the relative's room whilst they *stabilised me*. As the curtains shut, I saw that the resus trolley had been moved to outside my bay.

The nurses started tugging at my layers.

'Your temperature is unreadable, Kayleigh. We need you to take this off,' said one of the nurses.

'No, I am cold,' I replied. 'Please, don't,' I begged.

They pulled off my pyjamas, dressing gown and duvet, and they gave me a hospital gown for my modesty. My whole body started shaking with the rigours.

'Please give them back to me, I am so cold,' I begged.

My head was swimming with dizziness, confusion and a feeling of doom. I had no idea what was happening, but I did not like it at all.

'Kayleigh, we think you have sepsis. Your blood pressure is very low, your heart rate is very high, and you have a fever. We are going to stop your TPN for now, and will need to cannulate you. We need to give you paracetamol to bring the temperature down.'

I had no clue what they were talking about. What was sepsis? All I heard was 'we need to cannulate'. Three different doctors grabbed a limb and started trying to cannulate me. They tried over 20 times, but my already awful veins had shut down due to the infection. It was made more complex due to my irretractable shaking (due to the fever).

Again and again, they stabbed me. They even started looking at my neck. They decided to get the anaesthetist. I must have been ill, because he came straight away. The fever had also caused my skin to be so sensitive, every stab felt more painful than usual.

I had tears in my eyes. I didn't understand what was happening to me, and I felt ill, really ill. The sense of impending doom was worsening the situation, and the vulnerability I was feeling was immense.

I eventually had a cannula placed, and they gave me paracetamol, which broke my fever. Slowly, each doctor and nurse left my bedside, until it was just my ward nurse. Dad was allowed back into my bedside after one of the doctors spoke to him. My pulse had come down, and the shakes or rigours, as the doctor had called them, had gone.

The nurse allowed me to have a sheet to lie under instead of my duvet. Dad kissed me goodbye. He explained that he had spoken to Mum and she was going to stay with me tonight, and that he needed to be home for Sarah. So, he left.

I lay on my bed and looked up at the ceiling, just processing what had happened.

I was diagnosed with septic shock due to my Hickman line getting an infection that then went into my bloodstream. Septic shock is when the body reacts to the infection. It's life-threatening.

I was having hourly observations and kept being woken up. Mum came into the ward all frantic and worried. When she saw me, she calmed down.

I thought to myself, *if Mum's not worried, nor am I.*

She got out of the camp bed and promptly fell asleep.

Around four hours later, I woke up really needing the toilet, had a bag of fluid running through my cannula, which must have been put up whilst I was asleep. It was night-time now and all the lights were off, with only the humming of oxygen and drips beeping in the background. I tried to move my drip stand to go, but accidentally woke Mum up.

She helped me untangle myself from her camp bed and helped me walk down to the toilet. On my way back to bed, the world started spinning, and I said to Mum that I needed to sit down.

She helped me sit on a chair by the Christmas tree, which was by the nurses' station. Everything went black. I did not lose consciousness, but I lost my vision, and I was terrified.

'I can't see,' I said to Mum.

She responded, explaining that it was okay and that it would come back if I stay seated. Mum comforted me as I sat. Things slowly started returning, first the Christmas lights, then the shape of the Christmas tree, then the outlines of everything before my vision was restored, and Mum helped me walk back to my bed. Where I fell straight to sleep.

The next morning, during the doctor's round, the ward consultant, who was the specialist in cystic fibrosis, was the lead doctor this week. I had not dealt with him often; he was not regularly on the ward rounds, so I actually spoke to him around once every six weeks.

He was tall, much taller than the other doctors, and he had thick brown hair that matched his eyes. He had an air of strictness but with an element of kindness. I only really saw him more when there was a CF kid in my bay, but they usually got side rooms.

Today, during the ward round, it was he and another doctor who was an FY2 or a foundation year doctor. I referred to them as baby doctors. He repeated what was said the day before: stop TPN, keep trying feeds and await GOSH. That was my life.

He informed me that I had been septic and that the infection I had was a particularly nasty fungus, but that we would know more about it in the next few hours. He explained that I would need antibiotics and a fungal IV, but that they would need to speak to microbiology to establish which ones.

I continued to feel rubbish, although better than I had felt the night before. Due to the infection, I was no longer allowed TPN temporarily until I finished the antibiotics, as the TPN could provide nutrients to the bug, making the situation worse.

I was back surviving IV fluids and Peg-J feeding again. I felt nauseous and tired. My whole body was sore; I felt like I had run a marathon. I had been allowed my duvet back, whilst I had no fever, so I curled up underneath it.

The teacher came around to say hello, and so did the play therapist, but I spent most of the morning dozing.

The consultant came to my bed after the doctor's round. This was unusual, as I was not a patient in his speciality. He sat on my bed and paused. He held both my hands, pausing again to look at them, and then he looked me straight in my eyes.

'Kayleigh, if you don't start eating, you will be dead by Christmas—'

That was all he said. He held my gaze for a few moments, although it felt like hours, then he placed my hands together and rested them on the bed, before getting up and walking out of the bay.

I said nothing to that. What could I say to that? I had been completely blindsided by it. Could he not see I was trying? I was trying every day. Even though I wanted to rip my stomach out of my abdomen every moment of every day, I kept trying to eat. It was the doctors who were not working hard enough to fix me. I was doing the best I could in this shitty situation.

This was one of my flashbacks: 'You'll be dead by Christmas.' I hear it spin around and around my head. Every Christmas was a bonus, and I see it as a bit of a f#@k you to him. Looking back at this now, it enraged me that a grown adult would speak to a sick 14-year-old about a topic such as her mortality, and worse, on her own, completely isolated.

It's a difficult conversation to have with an adult, let alone a child. I had been trying my hardest to eat, but I hated vomiting. I took the prescribed medication. I had all the tests. I had all the procedures. I never complained. I missed school, family, my sister, and friends. I was alone and isolated.

I didn't choose this, but it felt like he did not believe that, as though it was my choice. I was left feeling completely isolated and helpless.

As the day progressed, I was informed that my Hickman line would need to be changed after my course of antibiotics and a new one placed. My cannula was tissued, 1so I had that recited after nine attempts. My skin was not as painful now that my temperature had improved.

One of the doctors who had been on the ward round came back around 04:00 pm, and informed me that the medication I would need to kill this bug could make my heart go funny. So, during the first dose, I would need to be on a heart monitor, and I would need to have a doctor sit beside me for its administration.

I agreed, although I did not have much of a choice. So, a heart monitor was brought to my bedside, it was an old one, like the ones you would see from old versions of casualty on TV—a heavy box. Whilst I was hooked up to it, I received a message on my mobile, and the machine started alarming.

I was informed by the doctor to turn my phone off as it interfered with the machine. I texted Mum back, explaining I would need to turn my phone off and promptly did what he said.

As the nurse connected me up, it was like the ward was preparing for war; the resus trolley was moved back up to my bedside. A doctor I had never met before sat next to me with a white coat and stethoscope; he wasn't a children's doctor, as routinely none of them wore lab coats, except the consultants, on the ward.

The nurses fussed around me, checking in on me, making sure I was okay, as the antibiotics dripped into me. I felt fine, and the anticipation in the air settled. After the infusion, I had my observations checked, and I was unhooked from all the machines. They moved the resus trolley back by the nurse's desk, and the doctor left.

To be honest, the doctor was not very chatty, and it was very awkward with him sitting next to me. I was also not good at polite conversation. We primarily just sat in silence. Awkward silence.

The following morning, the doctors came around, just like normal, as though he had not told me about my mortality. They confirmed that I would need seven days of antibiotics, and then my line would need to be changed. As I would not be able to have my TPN over this time, they needed to continue with daily weights. I hated this.

Every morning, I had started experiencing anxiety before they would weigh me; they used to make such a fuss, as though I was not trying hard enough. They asked me if we could increase my feed rate a little. I repeated that it makes my nausea much worse, but they were insistent. So, I agreed.

In the back of my mind, I had Mum telling me that I needed to try, or they may go down the mental health route. I was so terrified of this happening again that any time I had difficult conversations with the doctors, it would be in the back of my mind. It was why I was compliant with everything, the cannulas, the tests, the eating, everything.

Like usual, the teacher came around and went. The play therapist came around with more Christmas activities that Harrods had given them. So, I sat on my bed and made more Christmas decorations. My nausea felt awful 9 out of 10; I was taking deep breaths to try not to retch.

I kept telling the nurses how sick I was feeling, and they kept telling me that I was doing well. The nausea was overwhelming. As the day progressed, I just lay on my bed; nothing could remove the crippling nausea, but as I was not vomiting, the nurses just kept saying I was doing well.

I was not doing well, not at all. So, I turned the feed down on the machine, back to my normal, which was about seven, and it would allow me to participate in life. I could not cope at this level.

No one seemed to notice. They disconnected me at 7 like usual, and because there was no TPN, I fell asleep at about 1 am like usual. That night, I woke up multiple times retching, but was able to fall back to sleep.

The next morning, the teacher poked his head in, and so did the play specialist. The doctors skipped me this morning, which was weird. I had been connected back to my feed, and it was back at my usual rate.

At about 12:00 pm, Dr Zhang came to my bedside and said, 'Kayleigh, we need to get more calories in you. The nurses tell me you put your feed down. Is that correct?'

Caught red-handed.

'Yes, I replied, but—'

'Do not touch my machines,' he interjected in a firm, almost scary voice.

'I could not cope, the nausea was too overwhelming, and no one was helping me.'

'We are all trying to help you, Kayleigh, but you have to help yourself,' he responded. 'We will continue with the IV fluids and feed and your usual. I can't believe ten mL more has such a difference.'

'Because I am only just able to cope with what it is now.'

'Well, we will just have to continue hoping you don't lose weight.'

I just nodded. There was nothing more I could say, and he left.

I felt really upset by this; it was as though they believed it was my attitude that was the issue and not my symptoms. That I was the problem, not my health. I started to panic that they were starting to go down the mental health route.

* * * *

The next few days came and went. Each day, amalgamated into one. My cannulas were tissuing multiple times a day again, and they were back to multiple attempts done by multiple people.

On Thursday, I was to have my Hickman line removed and changed. I was terrified following the last one. Thursday came very quickly, too quickly. That morning, I woke up, experiencing momentary happiness that I would be nil by mouth, so no feed. Then I remembered the reason for being nil by mouth, and my heart dropped.

I sat playing Sims for the morning; it was something I could use to distract myself from all the anxiety. The nurse came and gave me a gown to get dressed in, mum came at lunch, and dad came later in the evening. I continued to wait, I had fluids put up, and I spent my time walking up and down the halls just to get the nervous energy out of my body.

At around 07:00 pm, the porters came to take me down to the theatres. They pumped the bed up by foot and pushed me through the halls with the crumbling wallpaper. The halls were cold, and the nurses had given me a spare blanket to cover myself.

I was taken into the anaesthetic room where two anaesthetists were and an operating department practitioner (ODP). The ODP said hello but was busy and didn't stay long. The two anaesthetists were male and female.

The lady had blonde hair tied up under her blue cap and blue eyes with glasses. The man was older, he had grey hair, also covered by the blue hat and brown eyes. Both wore matching blue scrubs.

'Hello, Kayleigh. Today, we will be removing one Hickman and putting a second in, is that your understanding as well?'

I nodded. They then explained that I was not going to be put to sleep but that local anaesthetic should be fine for this procedure. I tried to explain that last time it hurt.

She responded, 'Yes, you will feel some tugging, but it won't hurt.'

Did all anaesthetists read from the same playbook?

They pulled my gown down from my shoulders, connected me up to machines and rubbed my upper chest with iodine. They draped a big blue sheet over me. This time they did cover me up, being careful not to expose my breasts.

'Okay, we will give you the local anaesthetic now, it will sting.'

I felt a sharp stinging go through my chest. They put the local anaesthetic around the Hickman that they were about to remove. They were going to place the new one on the other side of my chest. I looked up at both of them. I had started to feel a little nervous.

'I bet you don't have many talking patients, they are mostly asleep!'

The lady acknowledged what I said, but didn't respond.

The man just replied, 'No, not really.'

Silence again.

I held onto the railings on the side of my bed again, praying that it would not be as bad as the time before.

'Can you feel this, Kayleigh?'

I felt a sharp prod on my chest. I nodded.

'Oh, okay, we will give it a few more minutes.'

He started fiddling with the Hickman line, when suddenly I felt a massive pop reverberate through my chest. Then a pulling sensation, which vibrated through my neck. I suddenly came over really dizzy.

'I don't feel well,' I said.

I looked up at the ceiling and took some deep breaths.

'How are you feeling now?' the man said, whilst retaking my blood pressure.

'Better,' I responded.

My chest was very sore. I tried to look down, but the sheet covered my chest.

'Well, that is your old Hickman removed. Now we will put the new one in,' he explained.

I nodded my head and took another deep breath, and squeezed the bed railing.

'Local anaesthetic again, Kayleigh.'

The familiar sensation stung the other side of my chest.

'Okay, can you feel this?' he asked.

I could, but what was the point? Every time I had said yes, they went ahead with it.

I took another breath, and I felt a sharp stabbing in my chest, then neck. I squeezed the railing. Then there was pressure in my neck. The pain was unbearable, and tears flooded my eyes. I continued to hold the rails, my knuckles white. I felt a pulling.

'This may be a bit uncomfortable.'

The only way I could describe it was the sensation of stabbing through the fat across my chest; the pain was sudden, and it took my breath away.

'Ahhh—' I cried out.

‘Don’t worry, we are nearly done, Kayleigh,’ the lady said this time.

I felt them stab me again.

‘We are just doing the stitches now.’

My chest felt like it was bruised and on fire all at once. I had tears in my eyes, and my hands ached again from holding the side of the bed so hard.

‘All done, Kayleigh.’

I said nothing. I was in shock. It hurt so much. They moved the head of my bed back down, and I was pushed to recovery, where I had an X-ray to make sure it was okay.

I was taken back to the ward, and the cold halls were refreshing as I had gotten hot through the procedure. I wiped the tears from my eyes; I couldn’t let the ward see mental weakness. I don’t want them to think I was crazy.

I had to lie on my back for an hour before I could stand up. My Hickman line had been given the go-ahead to use, so the nurse came with my TPN and hooked me up. The nurse on tonight was always jolly. She had short mousy hair and blue eyes. She had glasses, but always looked over them and not through them.

She had a gappy smile. She chatted away as she connected me to the TPN. She went off and closed my curtains. When the coast was clear, I cried into my pillow. My chest hurt so bad. Why did I feel everything? I thought I was meant to be pain-free. When I eventually run out of tears, I lie on the bed looking at the ceiling.

Deciding that I needed to go to the toilet, I removed my bedsheets from myself and slowly pushed myself to a seated position to gather my thoughts and then stood up, being careful not to move my neck. So far, so good. I was still in so much pain, but needs must.

I turned to my pump to begin the walk down the hall, and my Hickman line fell from my chest in a heap on the floor. I looked at it, stunned, completely stunned. I could see the end of it and the feed dripping out into the puddle, onto the floor.

What the actual hell? I didn't know what to do other than I needed to tell the nurse, so I exited from my bay, and walked the four or five steps to the nurse's desk where my nurse was working.

'My Hickman line just fell out.' I said, still stunned.

She looked up at me, bemused. 'Sorry, what?'

'My Hickman line fell out,' I repeated.

She stared at me for a few moments and got up from the seat. She followed me back to my bed, where I had left the Hickman line still feeding on the floor.

'Okay, well, this is a tomorrow problem. For the time being, I'll call the doctor to give you an IV so you can have fluids overnight.'

I nodded.

I got back into bed as she cleared up my TPN, and I watched her walk away as I lay on my bed, confused, stunned, but terrified. I would have to go through that procedure again? I don't know if I could cope. I was still so sore, and now I had no IV access. This could only be problematic.

* * * *

In the doctor's round today, I was asked, 'Why did you pull it out, Kayleigh?'

I was shocked.

‘It fell out…I didn’t pull it.’

If they knew how awful the procedure was, they would understand that I would have never pulled it out.

‘Okay, well, we are going to have to reinsert it, Kayleigh,’ they replied.

My heart dropped out of the bottom of my stomach. I would have to go through that procedure again. I don’t think I could cope with that, but what was the alternative, death, like the doctor said? I nodded, but my brain was whizzing away, reliving the previous two insertions.

I thought that was the end of the doctor’s round, as some of the doctors started walking away.

‘Kayleigh.’

I looked up to see one of the other consultants looking at me. The hairs on the back of my neck pricked up. I acknowledged him, and he continued, ‘You were under someone called Kate, were you not?’ he questioned.

I nodded.

Where was this going? I thought to myself as I started to tense up.

‘My understanding was that you chose not to see her anymore.’

I nodded.

‘So, she referred you for a specialist assessment with a feeding and eating disorders team.’

I felt like I was being punched in the stomach.

‘What…W…Why?’ I stammered.

‘She was concerned when you stopped seeing her. When you attend GOSH for the specialist tests, you and your family will also be assessed by the top feeding and eating disorders team in the country.’

‘I don’t understand, why…I am physically sick!’ I argued with tears in my eyes; this was literally my nightmare that I was reliving. ‘I have had three assessments already, and it was proven I had physical symptoms.’

He looked at me calmly and said, ‘I think this is a good idea.’

That felt like a stab in my heart. The doctor walked away, and I could not breathe. I could not show weakness. I could not let them think I was mentally ill. So, in that moment I made a promise to myself that I was going to be on my best behaviour. To prove that I was not crazy. I was going to be the perfect patient.

I called Mum, who was working, and I never called, so it took her by surprise. I relayed what the doctor had told me, my voice breaking down and tears filling up my eyes.

‘I can’t go through this again,’ I spluttered down the phone.

‘I’ll be in later and I will talk to Dr Zhang, Kayleigh. Don’t worry, we will sort it out.’

Mum came and visited me in the evening. She gave me the biggest reassuring hug and asked the nurses if she could speak to Dr Zhang, and about an hour later, he came to my bedside.

‘Hello, Mrs Doran, Kayleigh. Do you mind if we speak in private?’

Mum nodded and followed Dr Zhang, who took her into the nurse’s office.

Mum queried why we were now going down the mental health route, and said, ‘Her symptoms are physical, not mental health. She has been cleared in the past. Why are we now wasting time looking at mental health whilst she has physical symptoms?'

Dr Zhang explained that it would be remiss if we did not look at all diagnoses, and this included mental health. Mum stood her ground, but Dr Zhang was having none of it.

'You have to work with us, Mrs Doran,' he said sharply.

Mum had no response. She stood there as though he had squeezed all the air out of her lungs. It took a few moments to catch her breath, but memories of the doctors threatening to take my care out of her hands filled her head.

Mum walked back to my bedside alone. I was waiting there with bated breath.

'I'm so sorry, Kayleigh,' she said, 'we just have to go through the motions again, but we have done it three times, we can do it a fourth,' she said stoically. 'We just have to be on our guard and not give them any reason to think it's mental health.'

Mum and I spent the evening chatting before she left to go home. She gave me a big hug and told me that everything would be alright. I was not sure I believed her, but I hugged her back.

The fight was on.

* * * *

I had the new line reinserted. It was awful, but I was being the perfect patient. So I did not cry or complain, I just let them do it. It felt like an assault, but I focused on the ceiling and held onto the bed railing whilst they cut into my skin. I had no choice.

A few days later, my aunty form Bedfordshire came down with my cousins. It was so lovely to see them. They brought me books and a knitting pattern to keep my brain occupied. I caught up on their life, and they caught up with mine. We went on a little walk and looked at the local shops.

I went for two walks in a day, usually, one with Mum and one with Dad. If I were hooked up to machines, we would walk the hospital corridors. If I were not hooked up, we would pop to the shops. I knew what was in the shops from memory now.

I showed my aunty all the Christmas decorations on the ward before going back to the bedside. It was visiting time, so the ward was all a buzz, but the ward sister came to my bed and said the ward was going to have some more special visitors. But she needed consent for that to happen. My aunty called my mum, and she answered.

'Your mum said yes, but only if you brush your hair!'

Apparently, when I had gotten into the paper before, all mum could look at was my unbrushed hair, and the excuse that I was a patient and not a model did not suffice.

I agreed but with reservations.

Over the next hour, the ward became very loud as the excitement increased and soon the guests were in my bay. Three members of the Fulham football team. They spent a little while with each patient. They gave them a wallet and a Badger teddy bear with a fulham footbal club logo on each of them, per patient.

When they got to me, I remember them being very polite but also a little awkward. Me being me, I chatted away, explaining a little about myself too. A lady then took our photo and provided me with a copy.

I still have that photo somewhere, my hair maybe brushed, but I was wearing a jumper that read boring, boring, boring, *down the front of it! To this day, I still have the teddy, photo and wallet.*

They wished me good luck and went on to the next patient, and I finished chatting with my aunty and cousins before they had to travel home. It had been so nice to have visitors.

Mum came up the next day and snuck me home in the car, and I had the loveliest of baths. It was beautiful and deep. It had bubbles and was so warm it felt like a hug. I hated the ward showers; I always got dizzy with them, so I was in and out, whereas with a bath, I would lie on a towel afterwards to regulate. *I actually thought everyone did this, apparently this was a Kayleigh-only thing.*

* * * *

In the days leading up to Christmas, I was able to go back to having a home leave during the day and come back to the hospital for TPN. Each day, I was excited for Mum to pick me up, and each evening I would beg Mum not to take me back. Since they spoke about the mental health assessment. I was terrified they were going to start treating me badly again.

Whilst I was there, I acted happy, and I said yes to all medication. I followed the doctors and nurses to the letter, and it was exhausting. However, Christmas was something to look forward to, even if it was going to be different this year.

On Christmas Day, Mum and Sarah came to the hospital to pick me up, as Dad had already gone to church. Sarah had not been allowed to open her presents pre-church as I was not there and was a little annoyed that I had got in the way of her and her presents.

We went straight to the 11 am mass and did all the normal church stuff, wishing everyone and anyone a Merry Christmas. People were asking after me, I was getting bored about repeating myself, but also a little annoyed that everyone felt they had a right to know about my health, even people I did not know. Was nothing private?

When we got home, mum continued to cook; the turkey had been started before I was picked up. Sarah and I were then allowed to open our presents. *I couldn't remember what I got that year, but I remember being happy with it.* We then watched a Christmas movie together.

Mum soon called everyone to dinner. I was not going to eat any of it today, I did not want the nausea to be bad. However, as we sat around the full dinner table, Mum and Dad announced that they had gotten me a special gift because I was not going to be eating. They passed me a rectangular box, which I excitedly opened.

'No way,' I squealed, 'GHD Hair straighteners. Wow!' I exclaimed. 'Please, can I be excused from the table to use them?' I begged.

Mum and Dad nodded.

So, whilst Sarah, Mum and Dad ate their fantastic feast, I straightened my hair.

Sarah always told me that this was probably the only time that she was really annoyed with Mum and Dad. She would have liked an additional present too. From her perspective, I took Mum and Dad away from home and away from her every day, when they came to visit.

Mum and Dad would buy me more CDs and PC games, and now an extra Christmas present. She was justifiably annoyed; I was getting preferential treatment. What she didn't understand was that things were just so dire throughout my illness that Mum and Dad would do anything to bring me some momentary happiness, even if it meant throwing money at the situation.

After dinner, I showed off my new straight hair. Sarah pointed out all the bits I missed and spent the rest of the day being annoyed at me. *At the time, I didn't understand why she was annoyed.*

The day moved along fast, and before I knew it, it was time to go back to the hospital. I begged Mum for five more minutes, with tears in my eyes.

'I am sorry, Kayleigh, it's time to go,' she responded.

It must have broken her heart every time she brought me back.

As we got to my bed on the ward, there was a gift bag at the bottom of the bed.

'That's not fair. Kayleigh gets two extra presents,' Sarah protested.

We opened it together. It turned out that Harrods also donated some Christmas presents to the ward. I got a teddy bear, which I placed next to the Fulham team badger bear, and some activities to do in the hospital and sweets.

Sarah eyed up the sweets. I was not going to eat them, so I gave them to her, which she was delighted about. I gave Mum and Sarah a hug goodbye before walking them to the exit.

Before we knew it, it was the new year. Mum, Dad and Sarah would be celebrating by attending the church's New Year's party. I would be connected to TPN and on the ward. It felt dire, but the nurses who were on that night were nice, so silver linings.

At 11:50 pm, the nurse came on the bay to see if anyone was awake; it was only me and one other child who was in a different bay.

'Kayleigh, come with me,' the nurse said excitedly, and I followed, dragging my IV line behind me.

She took me down to the day unit bay and into the doctor's lounge. The three nurses on duty were there, as well as the on-call doctors. They had a few snacks and non-alcoholic drinks.

We put the radio on and counted down the new year together.

'5…4…3…2…1…Happy New Year!' we shouted in unison.

As we did this, I looked out the window that overlooked London and saw hundreds of fireworks.

'Who needs to go to a firework display, when we can see 100s here?' one of the nurses said. 'They are so pretty, and we don't get cold watching them from in here,' she added.

It was really nice considering. After the fireworks died down, we were invited to go to bed. I texted Mum, Dad and Sarah a Happy New Year and went to bed.

* * * *

The new year started out just as the old year ended. TPN overnight, feed during the day. Pain and nausea.

I did not know what 2008 was going to be for me, but it could not be as bad as 2007, right?

On 9 January, Mum and I were driven up to GOSH by a hospital taxi. We told him a little of our story, and on the journey home, in the dark, he drove an extended route to take me to see all the houses with Christmas decorations. This was lovely of him.

In the appointment itself, we were informed what hospital investigations I would be having, and we were informed that we would be given an admission date, but until then, we were to wait with bated breath. We had everything counting on these tests. They had to tell us what was going to happen. Right?

It was now five months in the hospital and out of school. I rarely received homework from school. I had a history textbook, which I looked through, but as I had no access to the internet, I did not know what to focus on.

More recently, Mum and school were in contact and it was agreed for me to be referred to a pupil referral school for medical reasons, with the hope, I could get a tutor. The issue was that I was in a Surrey Hospital and in a Surrey School, but lived in a London borough.

The London council would not support a London teacher from the pupil referral unit going to a Surrey Hospital. However, they would support the teacher to go to a London home, so I would have to go home to be educated.

The plan was that I would finish TPN, get picked up from the hospital and go home. The tutor would come twice a week and, in the evening, I would be taken back to the hospital.

The doctors were still trialling medications with the hope of improving symptoms. Unfortunately, none had any significant improvement.

January became February, and this routine seemed to work. However, one of the new medications that I had commenced made me drowsy and caused me to dribble. It was so embarrassing. Due to the drowsiness, everything was much harder, and twice I fell asleep during tutoring.

It was Tuesday afternoon, and I was waiting for the tutor to turn up, but she did not. When Mum came back home after work, I informed her of this. Confused, Mum called the pupil referral office to find out what was happening.

She spoke to a posh-sounding lady on the other side of the phone, who read what the tutor had written in my case notes.

'Kayleigh is not interested in learning as she has been seen sleeping on two occasions,' she relayed over the phone.

Mum was outraged; she explained that the reason I had been referred was due to me being sick and that the medication was making her drowsy, but that I had done everything that had been asked of me, in spite of the drowsiness and nausea I had been experiencing.

The posh-sounding lady apologised over the phone and explained that she would speak to the tutor.

A few days later, we received an email from the tutor explaining that she was never told that I was sick, and she had not been told about my situation, but she was very sorry for what had happened.

It was then agreed that a new tutor would come to the house, who would be aware of the situation. She had curly grey hair, old lady glasses and smelt of humbugs. My medication was again changed, and I was no longer drowsy or dribbling.

* * * *

February turned to the beginning of March. There had been no significant change. Jake had been admitted to the ward and discharged, and so had Brodie.

I was still going home during the days and going back to the hospital in the evening, each day begging mum to let me stay at home. The ward had said nothing more about the mental health assessment, but I continued being the best patient; it was tiring.

One Wednesday afternoon, I was at home. Grandma had an appointment of her own, and she was not able to come down. (Wednesdays were her day as Mum worked longer hours.)

This particular Wednesday, Dad had a meeting that he had to be in-person for. So, I had the house to myself. Mum had given me a list of things that I needed to do, and to stop arguments on her return, I did them, dragging my feet.

One of the items on the list was to do my washing, so I was carrying the basket of washing in both hands and had my feeding pump balanced under my armpit. I was trying to carefully navigate the stairs when I caught my foot in the giving set and fell down the stairs.

I was in a heap on the floor, dirty clothes scattered around me. I had hit my arm, head and ankle, all of which were telling me they were unhappy. I lay on the floor looking up at the ceiling, thinking to myself that this was pretty inconvenient.

Slowly, I sat up, my usual dizziness happened when going from lying to standing, so I waited a few seconds to gather myself.

I slowly started picking up the clothes and putting them back into the basket. Picking up one of the jumpers revealed the end of my J-tube on the floor with feed coming out of it.

Crap, I thought to myself.

I looked at my peg and saw that the J-tube was no longer inside it.

'Crap, crap, crap,' I said again.

I knew what this meant: another trip to interventional radiology. I felt like I had failed at being the perfect patient. When Mum got home, I explained to Mum what had happened, and she took me straight back to the hospital.

They checked my injuries and made a plan that the following day, I would go down and have the tube re-sited. This took two hours, but they eventually did it.

I kept apologising. It fell on deaf ears.

* * * *

The same week, on Friday, I had been invited to attend GOSH for an outpatient investigation, an oesophageal manometry. It was a test where they put a little tube into your nose and down into your oesophagus. The test was designed to test the coordination and strength of the muscles in the oesophagus.

Mum and I were taken to GOSH again by hospital taxi. We had to leave at 6 am to get there by 8 am, and the night before, I had started my TPN early.

I had to be nil by mouth this time, so no feed was needed in the day—the only positive thing about having investigations. We also needed a nurse from the hospital to come with us. As I continued to experience weight loss, my health was classed as unstable, and GOSH would not accept me without a nurse.

Although it was an outpatient procedure, I was not in an outpatient setting, and I went into a ward that had lots of rooms coming off the main hall, and each room had what looked like very expensive and scary equipment. I was ushered into one of the rooms at the end.

A man with a white coat came into the room and explained what the next steps were.

'This test will take a few hours,' he said in a care freeway.

I nodded. Although I was not looking forward to this, at the back of my mind, I needed to redeem myself and be a perfect patient. So, no crying, no showing weakness, just focus on a spot on the wall, and that was what I did.

The technician put some lubricant on the end of the tube. He then put the tube into my left nostril, which felt like it was tickling my brain, and then I could feel it going down the back of my throat.

He told me to swallow, which I did, and after pushing about 30 cm of the tube down, he was happy. He explained that I needed an X-ray to confirm it was in the right place, and so the porter came and took me to and from X-ray.

When I focused on the wall, I used to feel this big barrier come up, like I was out of my body. The invasive procedure was happening to my body, but not to me. In later years, following my C-PTSD diagnoses, I recognise this as a dissociation, where one disconnects from thoughts and feelings.

The technician needed to push the tube down an inch further before sticking it to my cheek with tape.

The nurse who came with us had told us that her daughter worked at GOSH. Now that I was having the test, she was happy to leave us to go and see her daughter. Mum and I were happy with that as it was a bit awkward having a chaperone.

Over the next two hours, the technician told me to swallow different things and get into different positions, lying, standing and sitting.

After two hours, our nurse returned, and the technician explained the results of the test. He said that my swallow showed an abrupt constriction when food got to the lower part of my food pipe when eating and drinking. That I had a condition called dysphagia.

He explained that the lower third of the oesophagus couldn't be controlled (so they could not blame this on mental health), and the next steps were to recommend me for more tests.

Mum and I were happy with this result.

'See, it's not mental health,' she said to the nurse as we got back in the taxi.

That taxi journey home was the scariest I have ever been in. The driver seemed to rule the roads with his own rules, and on top of that, his car seemed to defy gravity, with the weaving and braking he did. I held onto Mum for dear life, and I could see the nurse in the front hold onto her seatbelt.

As we arrived in the ward, in half the time it would have usually taken.

The nurse turned around to Mum and me and said, 'Don't worry, I am going to report that driver.'

In complete shock, we both nodded our heads, stunned.

* * * *

At the end of March, the local mental health service reached out again, whilst they were waiting for this specialist unit to see me.

Mum explained that I was doing exceptionally well considering she has been hospitalised for the past seven months. I did not want to see anyone. I could not trust them. I was the perfect patient anyway and did not need mental health support.

It probably would have been a good idea if I had support, but we saw the mental health service as the enemy.

I had been asked if, during the time at home, I would want to go to school for a few hours. I jumped at the chance.

We went in for a meeting with my head of year. We spoke at length about the fact that I would need to drop many classes, but during my *free periods,* I could sit in the library, or I could sit in Mr Law's cupboard or in Mrs Rodgers' room.

I was not sure why, probably the number of times Mr Laws' cupboard was brought up, but Mum and I found it hilarious that this was offered as a place of study. I did go and see the cupboard, and I could confirm that it was a room.

The patients continued to come in and out, Jake went back to the hospice again, Brodie was admitted and discharged, but I stayed.

I woke up suddenly one Tuesday morning to the girl in the bed next to me, running through my drawn curtains, to the toilet. It turned out she had E. coli, and the same day, she was put into a side room.

A few hours later, I was having a CT scan and needed to have a cannula for it. After 13 attempts, the anaesthetist got a cannula in my foot. I spent the day gingerly walking on it whilst I waited to be called down.

In the test itself, they gave me something that they said would make me feel like I was peeing myself, but they promised me I wasn't. I did not experience this, but did feel extremely warm, like I was being heated by my blood vessels. I had the test and was taken back to the ward.

That evening, I started feeling really poorly, my fever spiked, and my pulse raced. It felt like sepsis again.

The doctors and nurses rallied around me, and I was given antibiotics and my blood was taken. They stopped giving me my TPN, and whilst they worked out where the infection was, I was back to cannulas. My veins continued to be horrible.

The dread on doctors' faces when they had to come and take blood or cannulate me, I felt the same, but didn't show it. I would just stare and the ceiling or wall and disassociate. This was how I got through it.

Whilst I had the infection, I was no longer allowed home, and the home tutor stopped, and I had only lasted three days at school.

When to doctors came for the doctor's round two days later, I was informed that I had grown E. coli in my blood. But that it was not in my Hickman line. They believe I got it through the cannula in my foot.

I had 12 days of antibiotics. At the end of the 12 days, I received a letter to be admitted to GOSH for hospital investigations. The date would be 21 March 2008—Good Friday.

* * * *

'What a weird date to be invited into the hospital,' mused Mum, Dad and a few of the nurses.

Yes, Easter was important, but this was more important. We had put all our eggs in one basket and hoped that GOSH could find out and fix me.

We got a hospital taxi again, and, in the morning, before we left, I found that Jake had been admitted to the hospital again. Mum came to the ward, and Carol wished us both the best of luck as we headed off.

This car journey was not a speedway racer, and I sat patiently in the back of the car, nervous about what the next few days would be like.

Scanxiety or Scan anxiety, a real and documented phenomenon for people with long-term health conditions. This anxiety was caused pre-, during or post-scan or test. The fear was real.

When we got to GOSH, we were brought to the front of the hospital this time, where they have the world-famous arch saying Great Ormond Street Hospital. I took a second to appreciate this moment before we headed inside.

Mum and I followed the directions on the letter and ended up in a quiet section of the hospital. It was not full of people; instead, it was quiet, not silent. There was no one behind the reception, and the lights were not even on. It was empty.

Failing to find any workers, Mum called the number on the phone and she got through to a lady.

'Our apologies, Mrs Doran, we have put the wrong month down, it is the correct days. It is April and not March.'

Although the anxiety resolved pretty much straight away, I was also disappointed that I would have to wait another month.

I tried to look at the positives; at least I had got out of the hospital.

The doctors had stopped letting me go home now, as I had lost too much weight and following the infection. I enjoyed this time off the ward, although it was a complete waste of time and money.

We waited three hours for a taxi back to the hospital. Mum and I sat in that taxi silently. We were both disappointed.

* * * *

Easter was quiet; the ward had been given Easter eggs, which I could not eat, so I was not bothered by them. As the antibiotics had finished, I was back on the TPN. Brodie had also been readmitted, and Sue made the joke that now that Jake, Brodie were in, the gang was back. Sue was like fresh air on the ward; she was so cheerful despite everything.

Over the Easter Holiday, Jake's room was so busy, he had back-to-back visitors. I was able to see him once in the room; he looked thin and tired. He looked unwell; he used to follow us with his eyes, but he was not doing that any more. The parrot that his dad had brought him was sitting at the bottom of his crib.

His room kept getting busy with people congregating in the relatives room, which was within earshot of my bed. I kept hearing that he had been seizing, and they were struggling to manage them. They were talking about how they were increasing his medication so he was no longer in pain.

I thought it was strange that the family was allowed to stay, even out of visiting times, especially as the ward was fairly strict with it. As Easter Sunday came to a close, I got washed, dressed and into my pyjamas. I wished Sue and Brodie a good night before closing my curtains, climbing under my duvet and falling asleep.

I woke up very suddenly. It was still dark, and I rubbed my eyes and sat up. I could hear that Sue had also woken up; I could hear her moving around. Even though it was the early hours of Easter Monday, there were lots of whispered voices. I went to check the time on my phone, but I had forgotten to charge it, so I connected it to the charger.

I lay back on my bed, placing my head on my pillow, trying to listen to the whispers, but they had stopped. In fact, the ward had become eerily quiet; you could hear a pin drop.

I thought to myself, *This is strange*.

All of a sudden, the silence was broken by a cry of true heartbreak, like someone had been mortally wounded. The cry went on until the last bit of oxygen had left her soul. The sob that followed was one of heartbreak, but worse. I didn't need an explanation to know that Jake had just died.

It felt like someone ripped out my heart whilst simultaneously punching me in the stomach. I felt like I could not catch my breath, as tears fell like a waterfall from my eyes. My brain could not compute; 2-year-olds do not die. No. I struggled for breath whilst sitting up, throwing the layers off me as I got too hot.

I must be strong, I thought as I took some deep breaths to regulate my breathing; my heart slowed with the gentle breath exercises. I lay back down to hear a tidal wave of tears coming out of Jake's room and the relatives' room. I do not understand.

I hadn't understood that Jake had been actively dying; I knew he was going to a hospice, but I thought he had years like Brodie. I just kept repeating to myself, 2-year-olds don't die. But they do.

Over the next few hours, the family left in dribs and drabs. Until it was only Carol and Pete. The porter came up to the ward with a porter's coffin, which was child-sized. I thought to myself, it should be illegal to make them; children don't die, but one had. Jake. That beautiful little boy with the big brown eyes.

About 20 minutes later, Jake's body was wheeled out of the ward. Horrific sobs came from Jake's room. It was heartbreaking. Carol and Pete left soon after. Carol could hardly walk with the grief that sat on her shoulders. She leaned on Pete, who was guided by one of the nurses.

The ward then went silent again. I don't remember falling asleep, but I remember waking up in the morning, and there was already a new patient in his room, and the ward was back to normal as though no child had died the night before.

Sue was the only reminder that something had happened. No one spoke to me about it, like I was just supposed to forget about it. In the days following, I heard about the funeral. I wanted to go, but I was not allowed as my weight had yet again plummeted.

On the day of the funeral, some of the ward nurses, who were not working that day, attended, Mum went, and Sue and Dave went too.

Mum went straight to work, whereas Sue came back to the ward with the off-duty nurses. She made a beeline for me and told me that it was a lovely service, that everyone was wearing blue. She showed me her dark blue bracelet that was on her wrist.

She told me it was very sad, but she was glad she went. She started to walk over to Brodie when she swivelled. She pulled the bracelets off her wrist and handed them to me.

'Have them,' she said. 'Something to remember Jake by,' she said before returning to Brodie.

I still have the blue bracelets, and I will keep them until I die. This gesture meant so much to me. Like I had a little bit of him to remember him by. In the nurses' office, there was a picture of Jake, that lived there for many years. I would like to think it was still there, but I don't know.

I found that many years later that Carol and Pete broke up after the death of Jake. It's so common for parents to split after the death of a child. As a parent, your child's death is literally the worst nightmare you could imagine, and they lived it.

I can still hear Carol's cry. It's one of my flashbacks. Her cry fills my brain just as clearly as when it was produced. It echoes through my brain, causing me to freeze and relive the moment he died. So far, no amount of trauma therapy or medication has stopped it.

* * * *

That was the day I lost my faith.

I had been questioning for years, I felt let down and betrayed by God.

All the prayers, begging God to make the situation better, especially for my family—Ignored.

All the prayers begged God to let me go peacefully—Ignored.

Over the years, I have had prayers in mosques, synagogues, different Christian denominations, and a Hindu temple. It didn't matter, I felt like all the prayers went on deaf ears, like there was no one listening. Like there was no one.

Instead, he made Carol and Pete, Sue and Dave go through the heartbreak of watching their once healthy child deteriorate and then die. Something no parent should go through.

I had now met so many children with life-limiting diseases, children who suffer every day, including me, and he provided no cure or respite. I couldn't fathom a hateful God, especially as the one I learnt about was loving and kind. I was so angry at him. The anger I felt was all-encompassing.

I looked over at Brodie and Sue, and it dawned on me that Sue was going to be Carol one day. I felt as though a vice clamped onto my heart. My little brain could not fathom so much grief. The only option in my brain was that there was no God, and it was just dumb luck or unlucky, as the case may be.

I lay in my bed looking up at the ceiling, and I suddenly felt very alone in the world.

These feelings were complicated. If you asked me now, I would probably say I am culturally Catholic. It was so ingrained in me throughout my younger years that to completely separate myself from it would mean losing parts of me. I don't really know what I believe anymore, and I am okay with that. I am also not searching for a deity either.

* * * *

For two weeks, St Alice's Hospital were having its windows changed out to ones that don't let the wind go through them. This meant that they were shutting down a bay at a time temporarily. The ward decided that they were going to transfer me to their sister hospital for a week whilst this was being done.

I packed all my stuff up and headed over to Hollyfield Hospital. It looked slightly newer than St Alice's; there was less paint chipping, and it had aged better than St Alice's.

I was very nervous to go to the new hospital, as it also meant new nurses and new doctors. It meant my case was being looked at by new eyes and that we didn't know what they were going to do.

The first night we were there, Mum ordered a pizza, now I could not eat the base of the pizza and the dough would stick in my throat, but the toppings are the best bit anyway. We asked the nurses if they wanted anything and brought them a pizza too.

Mum and I watched a movie whilst eating the pizza before she left to go home. Like always, I was sick into a vomit bowl and chucked it away.

In the morning, the doctors came around and told me that I was being discharged. I was confused.

'Why are you discharging me?' I asked.

She explained that the nurses told her that I ate a pizza, but there was no mention of you vomiting. If you could eat a pizza, you no longer need to be admitted. I explained that I had vomited and placed the vomit bowl in the bin; it was probably still there if she wanted to look.

That vomiting was second nature to me; we don't make a drama out of it. She apologised and I stayed admitted. It also turned out that everyone who ate that pizza got a stomach bug, including Mum. I, on the other hand, was absolutely fine!

I stayed at this ward for five days before being transferred back to St Alice's. Nothing much more of note happened.

****

As I settled back into St Alice's, there was a new patient in the bed next to me. . She was four years younger than me and had kidney problems. She had mid lenth brown hair and was fairly chatty. I got to know her and her mum over the next few days. On the third day of admission, her sister came up after school, wearing my school uniform, They went to my school! It felt like I had not seen the uniform in ages.

The sister and I got to chatting and I found out that she was in my year at school. What a coincidence. She was a very pretty girl with long ginger hair down her back with clear blue eyes and ginger freckles. She was extremely confident, too. Her name was Michelle.

Michelle and I spent her whole visit chatting whilst her sister was talking to her mum. It felt like we had known each other for ages. The conversation kept flowing. I was sad when her sister was discharged two days later, it meant that I had lost my friend. She was a glimmer of normalcy.

Michelle adopted me as a friend on that day.

Michelle and I stayed in contact, and she became one of my closest friends. Through Michelle, I met Lilly (who also went to the same school), who became one of my other closest friends.

****

At the beginning of April, I had yet another line infection. This time, the bug was a staph epidermidis. I had a fever and my heart rate raced. I was not as sick as the other times, but I noted that each time I got an infection, my body became weaker and weaker.

I was now not allowed to go for walks with Mum and Dad; instead, I had to be pushed in a wheelchair. I was so weak and the weight loss was so severe, it was to avoid any undue exercise to prevent further weight loss.

One Saturday morning, Mum and Sarah came up early, and Mum explained that she was getting her haircut at our usual place, and the hairdresser was asking about her daughters.

She explained the situation, and he offered to come into the hospital to give me a haircut as I was no longer allowed out. My hair had grown long, and I predominantly tied it in a ponytail.

I was very excited, I liked my hairdresser, and was looking forward to seeing him. He looked very alternative with a hole in his ear and lots of face piercings as well as on his ears. He had a sleeve of tattoos on both arms and up onto his neck, and you could see them poking out of his collared shirt.

Mum and I washed my hair and then brushed it out before he arrived. The nurses were excited on my behalf to get a haircut too, and helped put sheets out to catch the hair.

He came at about 02:00 pm, and when he saw me, his face dropped. I thought he realised that his face dropped, because he went over the top with trying to back track. I know I looked skeletal.

I know that my hair was falling out because of the lack of nutrition. He made a complete fuss of me. For that hour, I felt like a princess. I am forever thankful to him for bringing me some joy in this admission.

Brodie was back this weekend. This was going to be a short admission; they were changing some of her medication. It was nice to see Sue and Dave again. That was a memory that Jack was real, that he was a part of our lives. I could talk about him.

I had a radioactive test today where they put some radioactive liquid into me and hoped for the best. The scan anxiety was real, so I did not want to hear the outcome. I was taken back up to the ward and was sitting there waiting for my laptop to turn on when Sue came hurriedly into our room.

She looked at me and cried out with happiness, 'Kayleigh, I'm pregnant.'

I was thrilled for her. She looked so unbelievably happy.

'I have literally just done the test, I can't believe it…I am pregnant.'

She came over to hug me, and I shouted at her, 'DON'T COME NEAR ME…I'M RADIOACTIVE!'

Instead, we danced on the spot. I was there when she told Dave, and watched him break down with happiness.

* * * *

The antibiotics were finished the day of my GOSH admission. My bed at St Alice's would still be mine when I got back. We travelled up again in a taxi for the admission. We went to the same place we had gone to before, but this time it was a buzz with people.

They sat us next to these huge windows that look out onto offices. A nurse was soon with us and checking my observations. Once Mum and I had gone over the paperwork with the nurse. I was pushed up to a ward in a wheelchair.

The ward had bright colours, and I remember seeing all these new toys; St Alice's paled in comparison. The ward I was on was mixed, full of lots of interesting people. I made friends with a girl with neurofibromatosis; she had multiple growths over her face, head and neck.

She had her own room and her mum was able to sleep on a pull-down bed. We were informed that Mum would need to stay in McDonald's house (yes, that McDonald's), as there was no space by my bed.

I did not spend any time settling into the ward. On 24 April, I had a gastric emptying test. They had many attempts to get fluid into my stomach. They tried that I eat at first, and I vomited. They put the radioactive liquid straight into my peg and I partially vomited, but when they scanned later in the day, it had not moved out of my stomach.

I was informed by the specialist that I had a condition called gastroparesis. It was when the stomach does not empty properly and which causes nausea, vomiting, pain, bloating and feeling full. All symptoms I had been experiencing.

The next test I had was another endoscopy, with multiple biopsies. The endoscopy procedure was similar to the process at St Alice's. The only difference was that the young kids could drive these electric cars to the theatres.

I momentarily wanted to be younger, as these looked fun. When I woke up from the anaesthetic, I had a tube down my nose. This tube went all the way into the bowel and was for my third test.

The third test case was called a gastro-duodenal manometry. In a normal person, when they eat, their stomach and bowel contract like a Mexican wave. This was called the peristalsis. This test checked and made sure it worked okay.

They took me to one of the little rooms off the corridor. It had blue walls and a matching floor. There was an expensive-looking computer-looking thing next to a couch. The technician brought an uncomfortable-looking chair in for Mum. I was ushered onto the couch.

'Make yourself comfy. You will be here a number of hours,' said the technician.

I nodded and lay down. He connected the end of my tube to his computer.

'Unfortunately, you will have to stay as still as possible whilst we do the test. You will be here a few hours, and if you need the toilet, you will have to use a bedpan.'

Absolutely not, I thought to myself.

I followed his instruction and lay down on the couch, it wasn't particularly comfortable, but I had to make do. He asked for the end of the tube, and I passed it to him. He was Middle Eastern looking with thick-rimmed glasses on top of his brown eyes and nasal hair. He connected the tube to the computer and fiddled with it.

'Okay, Kayleigh, it's all ready,' he said after about five minutes. 'I will come in and out to check on you. If you need anything, just press the nurse call button.'

I looked at the computer and saw what looked like lots of squiggles. He smiled at Mum and me as he left the room.

Mum and I chatted for about an hour before our conversation died down. Mum then decided to pop to the shops to get a trashy magazine. The first hour came and went.

I snoozed on the bed and Mum read through her magazine. I started to need the toilet, but like hell was I going to use a bedpan, so I stayed quiet. The second hour came and went.

The technician poked his head in and asked if we were okay. Mum and I nodded our heads. He fiddled with the computer before leaving again. I picked up one of the magazines and started reading it. The third hour came and went.

By the fourth hour. My bladder was shouting at me, and I was very uncomfortable.

I thought to myself, *My bladder will have to burst before I use a bedpan.*

I suddenly experienced a wave of nausea and said to Mum, 'I feel sick.'

Then, I retched. This coincided with the lines on the machine going from being flat to spiking. Something had happened, but we did not know what.

I continued to stay still until the technician came into the room about 30 minutes later. We explained what had happened. He fiddled with the computer and suddenly got really excited. He showed us the computer screen and said that a normal bowel should contract from left to right, but in my case, it contracts from right to left.

'You have a condition called retrograde peristalsis,' he said with confidence.

'Is that why my tubes don't sit in my bowel?' I asked.

He nodded his head.

I could not believe it, I had a proper diagnosis, it wasn't all in my head, I told them! Not only that, but I was told by the best children's hospital in the UK. It felt like a weight had been lifted off my shoulders. That night I slept the best I did the whole admission.

I went back to St Alice's the following day. I was welcomed back, and even the nurses were excited on my behalf with my diagnosis. Gastroparesis and retrograde peristalsis. Just wow!

* * * *

With the staff at St Alice's, I had a mostly good therapeutic relationship. Although some days were harder than others, the staff were generally happy for me to get my diagnosis. As I had been there for eight months now, I thought they had just got used to seeing me every morning.

From the very cheerful cleaners who moved all the beds around in the morning to clean the floors. One of the cleaners was going through her own health journey and kept me updated with everything. To the nurses, bringing me home a gift after their trips abroad.

One brought me a camel from Egypt, and another brought me some cat socks that had been designed by an artist. One of the nurses brought me a beautiful necklace too, from a holiday. There was only one nurse whom I did not particularly bond with. I thought our personalities were too different, and that was okay.

I still have these gifts.

Since arriving back from GOSH, there was no talk about increasing feed anymore. These diagnoses proved that I had the symptoms. I did not have to justify why I was struggling. Having a diagnosis proved that I was not lying or being difficult.

Dr Zhang came to visit me a few days later. He had asked Mum to come up for the doctor's round too, and she sat next to me whilst Dr Zhang explained the situation.

'Kayleigh, Mrs Doran, it's nice to see you both,' he said. 'I have been in contact with GOSH and they have told me of your diagnosis.' This is brilliant news! We have spoken at length about how best to treat this.

'Unfortunately, all the medications that may help, you have already trialled with no significant improvement, and there is no known cure for this condition.'

In that sentence, my happiness bubble was burst. I felt a lump in my throat, and tears came to my eyes.

'There is an experimental surgery called a gastric pacemaker, but we do not know how effective it will be, and it's only been done in adults.'

I felt like I had been stabbed in my stomach. I looked over at Mum; she looked determined.

As Dr Zhang left, Mum looked and me and said, 'I don't care how, you will be getting that surgery.'

She kissed me on my cheek and left the ward. I knew when she went home, she would do a deep dive into all things gastroparesis.

* * * *

29 April. My Birthday. I woke up to a sinking feeling, and I was still in the hospital. No miracle for me. Carol's screams echo through my head, and I shake my head to shake it out.

'You'll be dead by Christmas,' popped into my head.

I shook my head again. My stomach felt like it was by my feet.

My machine started beeping. TPN had finished. I wait for the nurse to turn it off and disconnect me.

'Good morning, Kayleigh,' she says cheerfully.

I smiled, but my head was whizzing at 100 miles an hour. I have started feeling really alone, even though I have been surrounded by people.

'There is no cure,' popped into my head, then 'experimental treatment.'

I shook my head again as I pulled off my covers.

I sit at the edge of my bed and look at my phone. Mum, Dad, and Sarah have messaged me, wishing me a happy birthday. None of my friends have, though, I thought they have forgotten about me, as though I no longer exist.

Why should they remember me? I was never there. How was I going to catch up with school? How was I going to become a nurse?

I took a big sigh and stretched. I collected my toiletries and day clothes and, like Groundhog Day, went to the bathroom to change and wash.

I came back and made my bed. I sat on top of the duvet waiting for the doctor's round. When they saw me, they just repeated what was said yesterday. Groundhog Day.

The teacher came into the bay and said hello. He asked after me.

'No change, still here,' I responded, just like I said yesterday and would say tomorrow.

The play specialist, came and said hi. She offered me some arts and crafts. I politely declined.

The nurse came to connect me up to my feed, whilst I turned on my laptop. It felt like a Sims day today, something I could do mindlessly; it stopped my brain replaying every traumatic event that I had been exposed to.

It hit around 11 am and the ward went suspiciously silent. I didn't think much about it.

'Happy Birthday to you…Happy Birthday tooo youuu…Happy Birthdayyyy dear Kayleigh…Happy Birthdayyy too youuu,' the ward erupts in song: the ward doctors, the nurses (including two that were not working), healthcare assistants, cleaners, housekeepers and some patients all crowd my bedside.

They brought in a chocolate cake (without candles). I looked back at their smiling faces, and I couldn't help but smile. Some of the ward staff had put money together and brought me a little bag. It was so sweet of them.

The cake was cut and shared among the staff and patients. I picked at the icing; I was not able to eat the cake because of the dysphagia.

The ward then continued like it was just any other Tuesday. Groundhog Day.

Mum and Dad came up together today and brought Sarah. I haven't seen Sarah for about a month. I had missed her, but she had things over the weekend, so she had not been able to come and visit. Her life went on, too. She gave me such a lovely hug. Mum and Dad joined in.

They brought gifts up to the ward, and we spent about an hour opening the cards and presents. I told them that the ward wished me a happy birthday and showed them the bag I got. It was soon 7:30 and they had to go, as Sarah had school tomorrow, and they hadn't eaten.

So I walked them to the door, gave them all a big hug before watching them go down the stairs through the door window. I slowly made my way to bed, my feed got disconnected, and I got changed. Then my TPN get put up.

Tomorrow it would all happen again, minus the happy birthday. Groundhog Day.

* * * *

I was septic again…fever over 42° C. Rigours felt like every muscle was trying to run a marathon. The heart was also competing in this marathon race. Apparently, one in six people with sepsis die. I have had it three times now…Am I living on borrowed time?

Mum kept telling me that she was watching her daughter fade away in front of her eyes. I tried my hardest to be strong for her, but my hope that GOSH would find and fix me was dashed. I couldn't pick myself up from that. I felt broken.

All the years fighting for a diagnosis, and now I had it, I find out I couldn't be fixed. The idea of having to live with the nausea for the rest of my life felt overwhelming.

They moved me into the side room, the side room that Jake died in. The doctors said that I keep getting infections. To help reduce these infections, they want to keep me separate from the ward and use barrier nursing. I worried it was because I was dying.

Mum came in today and informed the doctors that we had been invited for the mental health assessment for the whole family. That would be a nice day trip out. Apparently, Sarah was excited as it meant she got a day off from school.

I was no longer allowed to exit my room, and I was not allowed to go for my daily walks either.

Each morning, I watch the sun rise in the window on one side of the room and watch the sun set on the other side of the room. Each evening, I waited until I saw the moon and I made three wishes.

Please look after Mum, Dad and Sarah.

Please make sure that Mum, Dad and Sarah are happy.

Please, can Sarah do well at school?

I don't believe in miracles anymore, and so there was no point in wishing for a cure. I was not fixable.

I spent the next four weeks in complete isolation. Only Mum and Dad could come and visit me. Sarah was allowed to come up on weekends, but we were no longer allowed to hug. No other visitors. Each day, I put a smile on my face. With the mental health assessment looming over me, I continued to play the part of a perfect patient, but I was alone.

* * * *

I would love to say that this day came around fast, but it did not. Now I was in isolation, I felt every minute of every day. In some weird way, I was excited for the journey just to have some human interaction.

On 4 June, Mum, Dad, and Sarah came to pick me up from the hospital. I put on my nicest hospital clothes, making sure I looked presentable and put together. My clothes now hung loose over me as I had lost more weight.

We sat in the taxi, quietly, except Sarah, who chatted the whole way up.

I was so nervous, memories of being force-fed popped into my head. Memories of the doctor saying *there are ways we can feed you without your consent* were reminders that the doctors threatened to take my care off my mum and dad.

I knew I didn't have an eating disorder; it helped that I now also had a diagnosis. However, I knew I was mentally ill through the trauma, not an eating disorder.

It was only later in life, when I was diagnosed with C-PTSD, that I understood what the years of being sick had done to me. I knew the flashbacks and reliving were not normal. I knew that the dissociation was not normal. I knew that constantly feeling on edge and that I was not in a safe place, was not normal.

I knew it was mental health, but due to the trauma I had experienced, it was nearly impossible to ask for help and admit my symptoms. When I got the C-PTSD diagnosis, everything made sense. Although, like my physical health, my mental health was not curable with a magic pill. It was hard work.

We arrived at GOSH, we went through the famous entrance and looked for mental health and psychiatry services. I had a butterfly in my stomach.

As a family of four, we sat in the waiting room before a lady called us through. She walked ahead of us but was quite chatty.

She brought us through a ward and, in an overly cheerful way, said, 'If we accept you, this is the ward you will be on.'

I looked around, and it was a large ward. Against one wall were seven beds, and opposite were seven more beds. We walked down the hall in the middle. The windows had bars on them, and the doors needed a badge to get in and out.

Each patient in the bed looked like a skeleton. Some patients had NG tubes, and some were connected up to feeds. These were not my people; it was terrifying. I doubled down that I needed to be the best patient.

I thought Mum thought the same because she whispered to me, 'Those people aren't you, Kayleigh. You are physically ill.'

We were brought into a room with one-way glass and a camera in it. There were plastic chairs on it and white walls. Each room continued to need to be buzzed in and out. We sat in this room in silence whilst the chatty lady said she was going to tell them we were here, and she left the room.

Three people came into the room, one male and two females. The man had short brown hair and a blue shirt. He had keys on his belt that jangled every time he moved. One of the ladies had brown hair and eyes. She was wearing a dress that had a pink and blue banana leaf print on it.

The other lady was wearing brown trousers and a crème top over her olive skin, she wore glasses over her brown eyes and brown hair. She spoke with a Spanish accent and introduced herself as a psychiatrist. The gentleman was a psychotherapist, and the lady was a specialist nurse.

They introduced themselves and explained how the days were going to pan out.

First, they would talk to me by myself. They would also interview Mum, Dad and Sarah together. Then we would be assessed together. Following that, they would deliberate and give us their findings.

They stood up and showed Mum, Dad and Sarah out of the room. Leaving me in the room by myself. It felt like the butterflies in my stomach had grown claws and were trying to claw themselves out. I swallowed, shaking my head as though I was trying to shake the nerves out of me.

The doctor came back around an hour later and explained that Mum and Dad were on the other side of the glass, but it was only going to be us two in the conversation. She confirmed with me that I understood, I nodded my head, finding my voice, and I backed myself up, saying yes.

She asked me about my childhood. She asked me about my illness. She asked about family and friends. She asked me about the hospital.

Where I needed to, I lied through my teeth. I made my family and upbringing seem perfect and idyllic. Whereas in life, we had ups and downs. She asked about being bullied. I denied, even though primary school had not been easy. She asked about my parents.

I made them out to be perfect. Saying nothing about Dad's anxiety. I made sure that I kept eye contact with them. I smiled throughout. I was chatty. I kept reminding them about my diagnosis. I hid any ounce of crazy.

Mum, Dad and Sarah did the same thing when we were questioned together. They asked if there was any family history of mental health. We answered *no*, even though my uncle was schizophrenic and my dad had anxiety.

We worked as a team, batting away and shred of crazy. They needed to know that I was physically ill. Having walked through that terrifying ward, it just hammered home how important this was.

One day turned to the second, and I was questioned alone by the psychotherapist. Mum, Dad and Sarah were questioned by the psychiatrist. Then again altogether. It was us vs the world, and we were ready for it.

After the two days of questions, Sarah returned to school, and I returned to isolation. I was exhausted, but I felt like I had done good. The thing was, when they asked about my illness, I had been truthful. When they spoke about symptoms and weight loss, I had been truthful. When we spoke about how hard it had been, I was truthful.

The crux of the assessment was not lies, it was based on truth. Any signs that could seem like a warning about small lies. We could not go down the mental health route again. I was terrified; it felt like life and death.

We received the finding letter two weeks later. An actual quote from my assessment:

'She remained largely cheerful throughout the interview, at times, this seems a little out of place and considering her descriptions of how unwell she has been—they put this down to my mood being okay. I may have been too positive—She denied feeling hopeless.'

I learnt my lesson from Kate—all they needed to know was that I was fine, not that I had a constant replay of all the traumatic events that had happened in my life. I was guarded about how low my mental health was and how much I was struggling because I had learnt from before.

They came to the conclusion that I was not suffering from an eating disorder. A weight was lifted off me, and I could see the relief in Mum and Dad, too. This meant the doctor would focus on my physical symptoms and that we could draw a line in the sand.

* * * *

I continued to be barrier nursed, but I kept getting infections. At the beginning of June, I picked up a candida species line infection. I had the fever, tachycardia and general malaise, which needed a week off TPN, which resulted in more weight loss and a week of IV antibiotics.

On 12 June, I picked up staphylococcus epidermidis. This again caused the systemic symptoms and required a week off TPN and antibiotics.

Just as I restarted the TPN, on 22 June, I again had systemic symptoms and was found to have Staphylococcus Warneri. I needed 10 days of antibiotics and no TPN. This episode coincided with my G tube flipping up into my stomach and knotting itself. Dr Zhang was so impressed that my body managed to do it. I had an endoscopy to get it reinserted.

One in six people die from sepsis…I should be dead by now.

My education was zero. I had no energy. My hair was falling out. I still experienced horrible nausea and pain. The nausea medication list had been exhausted. I was exhausted.

My mum's fear of her daughter dying before her very eyes was happening. I was dying. Unless I got this pacemaker.

Mentally, I was struggling; being in complete isolation meant that I was not distracted, and I would relive my traumas in my head. I just wanted not to be symptomatic anymore. I felt completely alone. I felt my isolation in my soul; it was all-encompassing. I was alone. I felt Jake's soul in the room, too.

Dr Zhang had been in contact with a surgeon who attended the Gut Club. He was a gastric pacemaker specialist. He informed him how sick I had gotten and that my situation was dire. We waited for his response.

The home tutors discharged me, as I was no longer able to study at home, and they were not allowed to come to the ward.

June became July, and the specialist doctor agreed to take on my case. One afternoon, Mum, Dad and I attended an outpatient appointment in Chelmsford. We drove for two hours to a hospital in Chelmsford.

The outpatients were in porta-cabins at the back of the hospital. I remember that even though it was a hot day, the porta-cabins were freezing, which was probably made worse by the fact that I had no fat on my bones; I was skeletal.

We sat in the waiting room silently; the journey there had tired me out. I was just happy that I was around other humans. We got called in by a nurse. A gentleman in a shirt and smart trousers sat opposite me. He was Sri Lankan with brown eyes and greying hair. He had a nice smile and heavy eyebrows.

Mum and Dad talked all things pacemaker to him, and I sat quietly, only answering questions he directed to me. He explained we would need to apply for funding, but once this was accepted, I could have the surgery, as it may make my symptoms better.

'It may make the symptoms better.'

Was that hope I was feeling…no, it couldn't be.

* * * *

Mum became a woman possessed. She contacted anyone and everyone whom she thought could help our plight. She was all consumed. The pacemaker was all she could talk about, and at the beginning of August, we got funding, and I was given a date for surgery.

I was to be transferred to the hospital on 18 August the surgery was on 20 August. The ward was buzzing; it was all anyone could talk about to me, but I was reserved.

What if it didn't work? I could not give myself hope. I would not allow it. As 18th came nearer and nearer, I started to feel nervous. I had major surgery before, but this was different.

On 17 August, I packed all my stuff up. I was keen to get out of isolation after three months of only seeing nurses and doctors, I wanted to see the world, and when I say the world, I meant Chelmsford.

That night, as they put my TPN up, I had that sense of dread come over me. It's okay, I was nervous about tomorrow. Then my temperature started rising, and the rigours started. My blood pressure plummeted. I called for the nurse. She called for the doctors. My TPN was stopped, and I was found to have another bug growing in my line. Sepsis again.

The next morning, I was feeling much better, and I hoped that I could go ahead with the surgery. The doctors came in asking to speak to Mum. I said she was at home and they called her. I called multiple times until her phone was no longer engaged, and she picked up the phone.

'What did the doctors say, Mum?' I asked her, hoping that the surgery was still going ahead. 'Was it about the surgery? Is it going ahead? Is it—'

'Surgery's cancelled, until you are off antibiotics, it's too dangerous.'

The phone fell out of my hand, and it felt like I had been sucker punched.

I started crying, hanging up the phone. I cried for all the days I had been in isolation. I cried for Jake. I cried for Brodie. I cried for all the times I had sepsis or infections. I cried for the life I was missing. I cried for all the patients who had been there and gone. I cried for all the days I had been a patient.

I cried for all of the days I had been the perfect patient. I ugly cried from my soul. The nurse came in to my room as I bawled my eyes out, and she gave me the biggest hug. It had been the first time I had a human interaction in three months, and I held her tight as I sobbed into her shoulder.

As much as I may argue that I was not a cuddly person, as a human, there was a basic need for affection, for touch. I missed it, I craved it. But Mum and Dad didn't want to touch me, like I were glass, risk of getting an infection. The nurses and health care workers were limited in touch, too, only when it was needed. I started looking forward to having my observations done, just to feel close to another person, as I saw no one else.

* * * *

Out of the blue, the ward had contacted social services, and they told us it was policy for someone in the hospital as long as I had been. We did not know if this was right, but as a family, we saw it as a later Doran issue. Right now, we need to focus on surgery.

I was given another date: 27 August. In the days leading up to surgery, only people who needed to enter my room did, and they had to PPE up. We were not going to have another infection. No hugs from Mum and Dad. The nurses had to be tip-top with their cleanliness when accessing the Hickman line.

25 August: No issues

26 August: No issues

27 August: No issues.

I had not packed my stuff up because I believed that it was all going to go to pot. I truly believed that something was going to happen, and I was not going to get the surgery. So, I didn't pack.

This caused a great argument between Mum and me, the morning of the 27th, as Mum then had to frantically pack 12 months' worth of items and clothes in one hour. Luckily, I had sent a lot home at the previous surgery date.

Dad drove us to Chelmsford, and the car was quiet in anticipation of the upcoming hours and days. Once we were there, we were put in a waiting room, whilst the hospital worked out what to do with me. Apparently, the children's ward did not want me as I was under an adult doctor, but the adult side did not want me because I was 15 and still a child.

This debate between the two went on for five hours, as we sat together with the worry that we would have to go back home. It was finally decided that I would be going to the adult ward, which was terrifying. I had been in isolation for the past four months, and now I was going to be in a scary ward full of adults.

I was shown to a bed right by the nurse's station, and Mum and Dad sat next to me. I looked around the room; they were all adults with so many tubes coming out of them; it was worse than I imagined. The nurse told Mum and Dad it was time to leave, but I did not want them to leave me here.

Unfortunately, there was no flexibility; they told me they would be here nice and early tomorrow for the surgery and that I would be fine. They told me they would have to call Sarah to check in with her, as she stayed with our aunty. Mum and Dad left to go back to the B&B, along from the hospital.

That night I got into my bed and pulled the sheets up to my ears, trying to drown out the noises, but it was like a medical rain forest with beeps, and buzzes, drips and drops, moans and cries—whooshed and banged all night. Not to mention the different smells, some more pleasant than others.

I did not sleep much that night. When the morning came round, I was just pleased to see my parents again.

My surgeon was called Mr M. He came in to say hello in the morning. He was a very straight-to-the-point man, and his consent was as such. He did, however, have a jolliness to him. The anaesthetist then came, and he looked scary. I was filled with complete dread. Luckily, I was not to wait too long as I was first on the list.

Being wheeled down to the theatres, I kissed my dad goodbye. Only one parent could come with me, and even that was a debate, but we reminded them of my age, and they were a little bit more flexible.

In the anaesthetic room, it was a different anaesthetist, a lovely lady with brown hair. She explained that I was to have an epidural and that I needed to sit on the side of the bed and arch forward. She explained that she was going to put local anaesthetic in, but I didn't bother to tell her it didn't work. I was so anxious I struggled to find my voice.

I felt the sharp stabbing in my back and the stinging. I then felt a second stabbing in my back and lots of tugging. Tears came to my eyes, and suddenly I felt a sharp lightning bolt of pain shoot down my spine into my feet. I cried out as my legs uncontrollably jerked.

'Opps too far…It's in though.'

She put some tape on my back and told me to lie on my back. I followed her instructions.

I held onto my mum's hand so tight as they gave me the formula to fall asleep.

* * * *

Four hours later, I woke up in recovery.

I woke up to a lady in blue, putting a catheter in me, moaning that they should have done this in theatres. She had not even shut the curtains; my lady garden was exposed to the whole of recovery. The only blessing was that the other patients were asleep, but they were male. I was mortified. I tried to move, but I could not move my lower body.

'Hello,' I said to the nurse.

She popped her head up and said, 'Ah, you are awake. I am just putting a catheter in as you won't be able to control your bladder with the epidural.'

I looked over to the other patients. I thought the nurse read my mind and went to shut the curtains. She finished what she was doing before unbending my legs and walking off.

I had oxygen on and heart monitors, and I felt sick, but that was normal for me.

I'm not cured, I thought to myself as my heart dropped.

I had spoken to Mr M before, and he had said we may need to change different settings to find an optimal one. I trusted what he said and focused on this.

I was soon taken to the ward, where I was Pat slid (where they use a big board) from the theatre bed to the ward bed. The two HCAs were both male, and they rolled me over with such ease, I remember feeling so vulnerable as they did that. Mum and Dad crowded the side of the bed, and I, on and off, snoozed for the next hour.

When I woke up, Mum and Dad were still there. Dad said that he had to leave to go back home to Sarah. He gave me the biggest of kisses and left. As we were having this interaction, I remember noting that I was in quite a bit of pain.

I should not have any pain, I thought to myself.

By the second hour, it felt like I could feel every knife mark that was made on me, and tears were streaming down my face. Mum just watched in horror as every time she touched me, I cried out in pain. The nurses explained to me that I had an epidural and should not be in pain.

They explained that this was likely me being groggy from the anaesthetic. I tried to argue I was in actual pain, but they were having none of it. Four hours later, there was no let-up. Six hours later, Mum could not even touch the bed; a simple touch felt like I was being stabbed.

My wound went from my diaphragm to my belly button, and a second four-inch scar on the right side of my abdomen. The pain was real. Eventually, the nurses asked an anaesthetist to review me, and an hour later, they did. He reiterated that I should not be in pain and left. I was beside myself.

'Mum, please, it hurts,' I begged her.

The staff decided that because I was having such a strange reaction to the anaesthetic and that I was a child, they would move me to the bed right by the nurses' station. It was agony. I felt like I could not breathe from pain.

Mum was beside herself, begging people to take me seriously. As the day staff turned to night staff, it felt hopeless. The handover between the nurses happened at the end of the bed.

When the night nurse queried about the pain, my day nurse said to the night nurse, 'I think it's drug-seeking behaviour.'

The night nurse came over after handover and said to me that I may be a little more comfortable on my side. She called a colleague over, and the two of them manoeuvred me. As they did this, they went silent.

Mum asked them what the problem was, and the nurse responded, 'It looks like the epidural has fallen out and has been infusing the bed sheet. It must have fallen out on the transfer eight hours ago.'

Very quickly, I was taken back to theatres, where a different anaesthetist placed an epidural.

I remember him telling me to cough to avoid chest infections. Had I not been writhing in pain for eight hours, I probably would have given him the time of the day, but all my f##@s, had been given, and he received an overly tired, mentally drained sob.

When it was replaced, I was much more comfortable. To cover up their mistake, they got the pain team down who prescribed these little fentanyl lolly pops. I have to admit I did like the fentanyl lolly pops. By day three, as I sat on the bed giggling my little heart out, they decided that I no longer needed them for pain, and they were stopped.

Whilst we were there, a lovely lady called Nicola was also having a pacemaker insertion. She was the first person I had met with the same-ish condition as me. She had a son and husband who completely doted on her.

We got through the next few days together, and soon, we were to be discharged. We exchanged emails and promised to keep in contact over Facebook.

Nicola and her family were such lovely people. When Mum was away getting dinner or going for a walk, they kept me company and looked out for me. We stayed in contact. Nicola had a really tough time, and her pacemaker did not really work for her.

Unfortunately, and heartbreakingly, Nicola passed away in 2024. I hoped she was now at peace. I had such fond memories of her and her family, which will be etched in my heart forever—a hospital bond.

A number of days later, I was informed that I was going to be transferred back to St Alice's Hospital. It would be by ambulance, and Mum was coming with me. I was a little excited to go back and see everyone, especially as they had removed my Hickman line as I was tolerating more feed. I wanted to show the ward staff how well I was doing.

My waves of nausea continued to happen, the retching and pain were still there, but the background nausea had become a little better enough that my feed could go a little higher, and this was enough to come off the TPN.

We waited 12 hours for that ambulance. When they arrived, they were so apologetic. We were not going anywhere; it was fine. They put me on a bed and wheeled me into the ambulance.

The driver explained that because they were running so late and they needed to work within their allotted hours, they had special permissions to go blues and twos. They asked if that was okay.

What a question? Yes, of course, I loved the idea! They sat me up so I could look out the window, but it was too dark to see much else.

We went over the Queen Elizabeth Bridge on sirens, and I felt very special.

At one point, we broke hard, and the driver said, 'Sorry! I ran out of road!'

Other than that, we arrived back at the hospital around 11 pm.

Both Mum and I were exhausted. She didn't bother going home, opting to sleep on the pull-down bed, as she didn't have the car to drive her.

* * * *

In the next doctor's round, we spoke about the importance of trialling the feed again and trialling some of the medications too. I agreed.

Everyone seemed really happy to see me. It was so nice to be home (well, hospital) and safe. The nurses made a fuss over me.

Social services came to see me. It was a lady in smart clothes with short, thick brown hair and hazel eyes. She asked me about my situation, and I sat chatting with her. I was doing well and was happy and relaxed.

The conversation lasted for 30 minutes. The outcome of the case was that it was closed. However, they did recommend a charity to contact for a holiday.

On my 365th day of admission, we were finally talking about going home tomorrow. I was so unbelievably excited. I wanted to go that day, but they needed to get things in place before I went home. I dragged my feet, but agreed to go tomorrow.

Today was my 366th day in the hospital, and it was my final day. I was now free to be me. The ward staff brought my take-home drugs and left them in a neat bag on my bed. I had seen this happen to hundreds of children; I could not believe it was happening to me. My mum came to pick me up at around 01:00 pm.

The staff, including the housekeepers, cleaners, and play therapists, came to say goodbye to me, each hugging me. The ward brought me a lovely gift as a good luck present. I felt so unbelievably loved and special.

This year had been so hard; there was a relief, but also a fear of the unknown in going home. Mum and I packed up my stuff and we went through the doors for the last time. I was homeward bound.

I was so excited to be at home. Mum had changed my sheets all ready for me. Sarah gave me the biggest hug when she came back from school. Dad was so happy to finally see his two girls at home. It was a bliss.

In the October half term, we went to Hafan y Môr in Wales, through the charity that social services had sent us. It was so lovely to have this long-missed family time. We went into the mines, went swimming and contemplated climbing Snowdon (we decided not to because it was raining and we were lazy). The family time was bliss and really needed. We became a temporary bubble of happiness.

* * * *

Being back at home, the bubble soon burst, and I found being at home really difficult. I expected it to be easy and that I would pick up where I left off, but life had moved on and I hadn't.

Sarah was now a teenager and had gained a personality. I couldn't understand why she rightly had opinions and did not agree with me anymore.

I had been institutionalised and was finding the freedom really difficult. I experienced a big change in my routine. I was not around adults all the time. I also did not feel the need to activate the fight or flight response that I developed from being in the hospital so much. This response had been triggered by my efforts to be the perfect patient.

It meant that where things did trigger the fight or flight, for example, Mum telling me off for not washing up, I would be *triggered* and overwhelmed. I started a new fight…C-PTSD.

I slowly started trying different foods. I was advised that they had to be thick or fizzy. For me, I had to be able to swallow them due to the dysphagia. I could not eat anything heavy or bulky.

I avoided hard carbohydrates. I could manage overcooked pasta with lots of cheese (more cheese than pasta), and I would still feel sick, but that background nausea was better.

I returned to school within a week. I was now in Year 11, and I had dropped many classes, intending to focus on the classes I needed to get into university. I wanted to be a nurse and so in the next year I would get four GCSEs with the hope that sixth form I could do a BTEC and the fifth GCSE.

The school went above and above to support me in doing this. Although I never used Mr Law's cupboard or Mrs Rodgers' room. I stayed mostly in the library.

Life was still plagued with symptoms daily, but being around people made life that bit easier. At school, I started hanging around with Michelle, whom I met through the hospital and through her, I found Lilly, and we just bonded like a house on fire and continue to be best of friends to this day.

The reality was that for a period of time, I did okay. I became adept at just having enough calories to keep my weight maintained. I would have a family-sized bag of Milky Bar at night, a Milky Bar during the day at school and tinned beans with sausages and extra cheese. I would still vomit, but not everything.

I would chase everything with a Pepsi Max as the pressure from the carbonation pushes food past the bit of my oesophagus that did not work, and I would vomit less.

It was not much, but it kept me out of the hospital. The sensation of warmth in my stomach was beautiful, a feeling I really missed. The nausea and retching afterwards were not fun, but I was eating and I was free. However, over time, my tolerance for my symptoms reduced.

I felt the nausea more. I felt the pain more, and no matter how often I changed the pacemakers' settings, there was no miracle cure. The symptoms continued until I could no longer manage them.

It took many years to work out what was wrong with me, but my final diagnosis was gastroparesis with intestinal dysmotility. (My stomach does not work, and my bowel also does not work or works backwards.)

I went on to be diagnosed with hypermobility Ehlers Danlos syndrome (EDS), a genetic condition that causes your connective tissues to be extra stretchy, which affects my joints and is the reason why I was so clumsy. It causes my fast heart rate, low blood pressure and dizziness on standing up, as well as allergies too.

I have asthma, where I am unable to breathe on exercise; fibromyalgia, which causes generalised pain; dysphagia, where I am unable to swallow properly and a diagnosis of complex post-traumatic stress disorder (C-PTSD) as my brain is traumatised from everything I went through. Due to the lack of nutrition, I also have a diagnosis of osteoporosis.

There was a belief from the specialist that my vagus nerve was injured/cut during my third mission, which caused the constant nausea, as I always had the waves of nausea from childhood. If you remember, at the beginning of the book, I had an endoscopy where chips were in my stomach undigested over 12 hours later.

At this point, I should have been diagnosed with gastroparesis. If this had been the case, I would have avoided all the mental health assessments and trauma.

I am not bitter…Okay, maybe a little bit.

Other than the asthma, fibromyalgia and C-PTSD, my EDS is the cause of all my diagnoses. The EDS symptoms are varied, and the best control of the condition is through symptom management.

The condition affects people in so many different ways that it's impossible to talk about progression or long-term outlooks. So, we take it a symptom at a time, and try and live the best life we can—that is all I could do.

I am not angry at my treatment *now,* but it took a long time for me to give up my anger. I also have to grieve for the life I wanted to. It was difficult. As a disabled adult, I have a lot of trauma stemming from how I was treated as a child and since then.

Therapies and mental health services have been really good in supporting me, but it was so hard to admit that I was mentally ill, because of the fear of being diagnosed as mentally ill. What a paradox.

* * * *

At high school, I got my five GCSEs and went on to get three distinctions in my BTEC A-level. I got into uni and went on to study adult nursing at the University of Surrey.

Age 21, due to my symptoms, I did end up back on TPN, but with the support of St Mark's Hospital's intestinal rehabilitation unit, I was able to manage my condition at home with parenteral nutrition. Life was not easy, but I made what I could with it. I climbed a mountain; I travelled as far as the Middle East and the US. I went skiing (which went badly!).

I completed my Gold Duke of Edinburgh. I got an allotment. I went on to study occupational health with Brunel University and received a PGDIP. *(I hope to upgrade it to a master's when I finish this book.)* I have worked in occupational health for the past 10 years, as a nurse and a specialist advisor, in the NHS and privately.

I got into occupational health through requiring support for my disability, as they supported me into work. I continue to be best of friends with Lilly and Michelle (*who helped read my book and spurred me on to getting it published*). I lived alone.

I have found my life partner, and we got a dog together. (*I am hoping there will be a ring this year...hint, hint.*) We hope to start the adoption process at the end of this year. We are about to buy a house too, which is exciting! I hope to get chickens as well.

Due to my conditions, I take each day at a time; that's all I could really do. I try and focus on the positives and try and laugh at the negatives. It doesn't always work, but I have surrounded myself with wonderful and strong people who lift me up when I couldn't, both literally and figuratively. Plus, I am on strong medication and therapy.

Thanks to the specialist team that has been keeping me alive for the past 10 years.

I have a life that I live to the best of my ability, and I show up for myself. That is all I could ask of myself. From my viewpoint, I have got the partner, the house and the dog. In my eyes, I have ended with the fairy tale.

The End

Medical dictionary

NG tube/Naso gastro tube – a tube that goes into the stomach via the nose.

NJ tube/Naso Jejunum tube – a tube that goes into the Jejunum via the nose.

Peg – a tube that goes into the stomach through the abdomen.

GJ Tube – where a tube is placed inside the peg. That tube has been placed into the Jejunum.

C-PTSD – Complex Post-Traumatic Stress Disorder

Dysphagia – difficulty swallowing.

Gastroparesis – paralysed stomach.

Peristalsis – involuntary constriction and movement throughout one's digestive tract.

Retrograde – backwards